1 & 2
THESSALONIANS
A SELF-STUDY GUIDE

Irving L. Jensen

MOODY PRESS
CHICAGO

Cover photo: The Acropolis in Athens, Greece

ISBN: 0-8024-4488-1

1 2 3 4 5 6 Printing/EP/Year 95 94 93 92 91

Printed in the United States of America

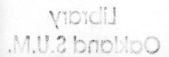

Contents

Introduction

Christ's first coming to earth was a crucial event in world history; His second coming will be the climactic event. He came the first time to die and be raised to life. When He comes again, it will be to gather to Himself those saved by His death. Paul sums up all the joys and glories of this ingathering by saying simply, "And so shall we ever be with the Lord" (1 Thess. 4:17). It is no wonder that the gospel is "good news."

Of Paul's letters, 1 and 2 Thessalonians focus especially on the theme of Christ's return. Here, the apostle not only gives the details of prophecy but he also shows how Christians should be living day by day in light of the Lord's return. You cannot study these epistles seriously without growing stronger in your Christian faith and service.

Some Suggestions for Study

Here are some suggestions for making your study of 1 and 2 Thessalonians most effective:

1. Studying by paragraphs should always precede verse-by-verse study, so that you will not lose your bearing in details of the Bible text. Paragraph-by-paragraph study is consistently fostered in these self-study books.

2. Meditate long over implied as well as explicit meanings of important words of the Bible text. Sometimes a single strong word in the Bible text teaches many vital spiritual truths.

3. Jot things down. Someone has said that the pencil is one of the best eyes. This is why it is so important to establish the habit of recording observations on paper, as well as making notations on the pages of your Bible. Throughout the manual, you are urged to record your observations. The analytical chart, suggested in some lessons, can be a productive worksheet for organizing your stud-

ies. This chart method is described in detail in the author's book *Independent Bible Study*.

4. Study independently. The emphasis here is always to see first for yourself what the Bible text says, then go to commentaries for help. Most of the directions of this manual are geared to encourage original, firsthand study.

5. The Bible is your textbook. Whatever version of the Bible you use, choose an edition with large print and wide margins. Also, make notations on the pages of your Bible as you study—underlining, cross references, notes, and so on.

6. Use different versions of the Bible. The King James Version is the one referred to throughout these study guides. In your study, work mainly with one basic version, but refer to other versions or paraphrases for the valuable light they may shed on the meaning of a word or phrase that appears unclear in the version you are using. Two recommended study versions are the *American Standard Version* and the *New American Standard Bible*. A useful paraphrase is *The Living Bible*.

7. Depend on the Holy Spirit to throw light on the Scriptures which He inspired. Meditate long over words and phrases that calls to your attention in the course of your study. Continually ask the question, What can I learn from this? Always have an eager attitude to obey God's Word to you.

8. If you are studying with a group, such as a home Bible class, consult other manuals of this self-study series for suggestions about group study.

Lesson 1

Background of the Thessalonian Epistles

This opening lesson is devoted to a study of the background and setting of the Thessalonian epistles. Many Christians think of these letters merely as two books hidden in the New Testament's twenty-seven—and the identification stops there. Your study of this lesson will reveal how 1 and 2 Thessalonians fill a unique place in the New Testament. Here you will acquaint yourself with such things as why the books were written, to whom and by whom, and why God made them part of the New Testament.

Your diligence in studying this lesson will be amply rewarded in the studies that follow. You will feel more at home in the letters, and this will make it much easier for you to apply the Bible text in your own life.

I. THE CITY OF THESSALONICA

A. Name

The city was originally named Therme. When it was refounded by Cassander, around 315 B.C., he named it Thessalonica, after his wife.

B. Location

Study carefully the location of Thessalonica, as shown on the map. Note the city's strategic position as a port on the Egnatian Way, which was the principal east-west trade and military route between Rome and Asia Minor.[1] How does this strategic location shed light on 1 Thessalonians 1:8?

1. Sections of this fifteen-foot-wide paved highway remain to this day.

6

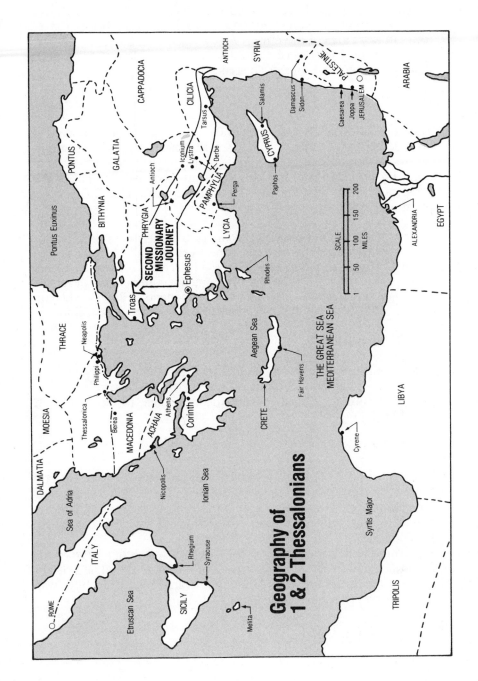

Geography of 1 & 2 Thessalonians

7

Observe the other two important cities of this part of Macedonia, Philippi and Berea, which Paul visited on his second missionary journey. Why did Paul concentrate much of his missionary tours in key cities of the empire?

Note the location of Corinth on the map. It was from here that Paul wrote both of the Thessalonian letters.

C. Population

The population of Thessalonica in Paul's day has been estimated at around 200,000 (about half its present population). Of this number most were Greeks, but there was also a fairly large Jewish segment in the city. From this description try to visualize Paul's impressions of the bustling city as he first entered it on his second missionary journey (Acts 17:1):

> With overland caravans thronging its hostelries, with its harbor filled with ships' bottoms from overseas, with old salts, Roman officials, and thousands of Jewish merchants rubbing shoulders in its streets, Thessalonica presented a cosmopolitan picture. It is very suggestive that the Jewish opponents of Paul should have called Paul and his co-workers "world-topplers" (Acts 17:6).[2]

D. Government

Thessalonica was made the capital of the province of Macedonia in 148 B.C. It gained the status of a free city in 42 B.C., electing its own government officials. (Note the reference to city rulers in Acts 17:6.)

F. Religion

Idolatry was the common religion of most of the Greeks. Nearby Mount Olympus, viewed daily by the people, stood as a symbol of the gods. In ancient times, it was at the summit of Mount Olympus that Zeus was believed to gather together all the gods of Greece for council.

The Jewish community of Thessalonica was either large or influential, or both, as seen from the action of Acts 17:5. The Acts account records the fact that Paul's first evangelistic preaching was done in the city's synagogue (Acts 17:1-4).

2. Charles F. Pfeiffer and Howard M. Vos, *The Wycliffe Historical Geography of Bible Lands* (Chicago: Moody, 1982), p. 457.

8

There was also a large Roman element, having a strong nationalistic devotion to the emperor, Caesar (cf. Acts 17:7).

II. THE FIRST CHRISTIAN CHURCH OF THESSALONICA

A. Paul's Evangelistic Campaign

Thessalonica was the second major city visited by Paul for an evangelistic ministry on his second missionary journey (Philippi was the first). Read Acts 17:1-10 for Luke's brief account of this ministry. Observe the following:

1. Upon arriving, Paul first told the gospel to the Jews in the synagogue. This was his customary procedure. How long did this mission continue?

2. Paul based his ministry on the Scriptures. What does the phrase "reasoned with them" (Acts 17:2) reveal about Paul's method of communicating the gospel to the Thessalonians?

3. Paul tried to establish three basic truths, in this order:

(a) Christ (the promised Messiah, Redeemer) had to suffer and die.

(b) Christ had to rise from the dead.

(c) The Jesus whom he preached was this Christ.

If you had only the Old Testament today, as Paul had then, how would you support each of the above three truths from those Scriptures? (If you are studying in a group, you may want to spend additional time discussing the subject.) For a starting point, see Isaiah 53.

4. Immediate results of Paul's ministry (Acts 17:4-5):

(a) Some Jews were converted.

(b) A great multitude of devout Greeks believed.

(c) A substantial number of leading women believed.

(d) The Jews who rejected Paul's message stirred up a riot.

(e) Paul was forced to leave the city.

5. Paul's later contacts with the Thessalonian Christians:

(a) Twice, Paul was hindered from returning to Thessalonica soon after his first visit (1 Thess. 2:17-18).

(b) He sent Timothy to minister in his place (1 Thess. 3:1-2).

(c) He wrote the two epistles.

(d) The apostle made at least two other visits to the area on his third missionary journey (Acts 20:1-4; 2 Cor. 2:12-13). Also he may have visited the Thessalonian church after his first Roman imprisonment.

B. Founding and Constituency of the Church

From the beginning, the newborn believers banded together in a Christian fellowship. What evidences of such a fellowship do you see implied in Acts 17:4, 6, 10? When Paul wrote to the group only a few months later, he addressed them as "the church of the Thessalonians" (1 Thess. 1:1). No doubt the organization of the local church was simple at first. We do know the church had leaders, however, as shown by 1 Thessalonians 5:12.

Most of the church's members were Gentiles, converted from idolatry (cf. Acts 17:4; 1 Thess 1:9). Some were Jews (Acts 17:4). From 1 Thessalonians 4:11, it has been concluded that for the most part the people were of the common working class. (See Acts 17:4b for a notable exception.) As young converts, the Christians at Thessalonica were a joy and inspiration to Paul, reliable and devoted followers of Christ. The bright tone of the two epistles confirms this.

III. THE FIRST LETTER TO THE THESSALONIANS

A. Author

Twice Paul identifies himself by name in the epistle: at 1:1 and 2:18. The title "apostle" does not appear in this letter or in 2 Thessalonians, Philippians, or Philemon. Some have suggested the reason for this is that any question of Paul's authority does not enter into the discussions of these epistles.

Silvanus (Silas) and Timotheus (Timothy) are included in the opening salutation (1:1). Both were intimate workers with Paul. Read the following verses concerning each man:

1. Silas: Acts 15:22, 27, 32, 40; 16:19-20; 1 Peter 5:12
2. Timothy: Acts 16:1-3; Philippians 2:19-22; 1 Timothy 1:2; 2 Timothy 4:9, 21

B. Place and Date Written

Paul wrote 1 Thessalonians from Corinth, where the apostle spent eighteen months on the second missionary journey, soon after leaving Thessalonica (Acts 18:1, 11). (Refer to the Appendix and fix in your mind the chronology of Paul's life and ministry. Note, among other things, when and where the apostle wrote each of his epistles.)

The date of writing 1 Thessalonians was around A.D. 52.[3] The epistle was among the earliest of Paul's inspired writings.[4] About how old was Paul when he wrote this letter? How old was he when he was saved? (See the Appendix.)

C. Occasion and Purposes

We have already observed that when Paul was hindered from visiting the Thessalonians (2:17-18), he partly made up for this by doing two things: sending Timothy to minister to them in his place (3:1-5); and writing this epistle after receiving Timothy's report about the church (3:6-13). (Read 3:10 for another thing that Paul did in behalf of the Thessalonians while absent from them.) This then was the occasion for writing 1 Thessalonians.

Paul had various purposes in mind in writing the letter. Some of the more important ones were:

1. to commend the Christians for their faith (3:6)

2. to expose sins (e.g., fornication, 4:3, and idleness, 4:11) and to correct misapprehensions (e.g., about the second coming of Christ, 4:13-17)

3. to exhort the young converts in their new spiritual experience (e.g., 4:1-12)

4. to answer false charges against Paul; such charges may have sounded like these:

(a) Paul was a money-making teacher, attracted by the rich ladies who attended his meetings. For Paul's replies, read such verses as 2:3, 9-10.

(b) Paul was a flatterer, with selfish goals in mind. Read 2:4-6.

(c) Paul was afraid to appear in person in Thessalonica again. Read 2:17-20.

Read each of the passages of this epistle in Table 1 and record the purposes Paul had in mind in writing these things.

D. Prominent Subjects

The prominent subjects of 1 Thessalonians reflect Paul's purposes in writing. Here are some of the major subjects:

1. affliction and persecutions of Christians

2. the second coming of Christ (the key doctrinal passage of the epistle is 4:13-18, the rapture of the church)

---

3. Some have placed the date as early as A.D. 50.
4. If Galatians was not the first to be written, as many hold, then the Thessalonian letters were Paul's first inspired writings.

11

Table 1

PASSAGE	PURPOSE
2:1-10	
2:14	
2:17-20	
3:6-8	
4:1-8	
4:11-12	
4:13-18	
5:1-11	
5:12-24	

3. thanksgiving for the Thessalonians' faith and endurance
4. encouragement to the church in their afflictions
5. exhortations to holy living
These subjects will be seen in the survey exercise of Lesson 2.

E. Characteristics

Paul's letters to the Thessalonians have the marks of typical New Testament epistles. They are like a doctor's diagnosis and prescription, blended together in one package. Some of the outstanding characteristics of 1 Thessalonians are:
1. It is intimate, heart-to-heart.
2. Its tone is gentle, affectionate, "a classic of Christian friendship."
3. The epistle is simple, basic.
4. There is an air of expectancy, especially concerning Christ's return.
5. The epistle gives one of the earliest pictures of the primitive New Testament church.

12

6. There are no quotations from the Old Testament. (Recall that most of the Thessalonian Christians were Gentiles, not Jews.)

7. There is not the usual abundance of doctrine in this epistle (4:13-18 being a notable exception).

8. Paul's style of writing is informal, personal, and direct. His style varied from letter to letter, as observed here:

> The style of a letter depends largely on the occasion that calls it forth. That to the Galatians, for example, is full of force, alike of argument and feeling. In parts of the Corinthian Epistles, Paul waxes warm, becomes almost passionate, denouncing his enemies and yearning over his children. In Romans he is all logic, though he soars at times, as in ch. 8. In Ephesians and Colossians he is carried along by the very majesty and glory of his exalted theme, though he is nowhere more simply practical in any of his writings. But in this Epistle [1 Thessalonians] he is fervent, simple, natural, just talking to his beloved children in the Lord.[5]

9. Much may be learned about Paul in 1 Thessalonians from the way he wrote and what he emphasized. Tact, love, and humility are three qualities that appear often in the epistle.

F. Place in the New Testament

As noted earlier, the Thessalonian letters were among the earliest of Paul's New Testament writings. Chart A shows their place in the multicolored spectrum of the New Testament library. Study this chart carefully, and you will have a good grasp of the diversified background of the twenty-seven books.

* * *

SOME REVIEW QUESTIONS

Before leaving this lesson, it will be helpful to review what you have been studying thus far. See how many of the following questions you can answer without referring back to the lesson.

1. On what missionary journey did Paul first visit Thessalonica?

_____

Name two nearby cities evangelized about the same time.

_____

5. C.F. Hogg and W.E. Vine, *The Epistles to the Thessalonians*, p. 5.

NEW TESTAMENT						
HISTORY	EPISTLES					APOCALYPSE
	Pauline				General	
MATTHEW	EARLY	LATER				REVELATION
MARK	during missionary journeys	after arrest at Jerusalem			JAMES	
LUKE	GALATIANS	FIRST IMPRISONMENT ("prison epistles")	RELEASE	SECOND IMPRISON-MENT	HEBREWS	
JOHN	1 THESSALONIANS	CHRISTOLOGICAL		PASTORAL	JUDE	
					1 PETER	
ACTS	2 THESSALONIANS	COLOSSIANS		1 TIMOTHY	2 PETER	
	1 CORINTHIANS	EPHESIANS		TITUS	1 JOHN	
	2 CORINTHIANS	PHILEMON			2 JOHN	
		PHILIPPIANS		2 TIMOTHY	3 JOHN	
	ROMANS					

2. What was the strategic location of Thessalonica?

_____

_____

_____

3. Describe the average Thessalonian in Paul's day.

_____

_____

_____

4. What was the religious situation in Thessalonica when Paul arrived at the city?

_____

_____

14

5. What were the main points of Paul's first sermons in the synagogue?

_____

_____

_____

What were the results of this ministry?

_____

_____

6. Where was Paul when he wrote 1 Thessalonians?

_____

Why did he write the letter?

_____

_____

7. Name some prominent subjects in this epistle.

_____

_____

_____

_____

_____

8. What are some of the letter's characteristics?

_____

_____

_____

9. When did Paul write 1 Thessalonians, as compared with his other epistles?

_____

_____

10. What key doctrinal passage appears in this letter?

_____

_____

Lesson 2
Survey of 1 Thessalonians

With this lesson we move into a study of the actual text of Paul's first letter to the Thessalonians. Our study in this lesson will be general in nature—survey study. It is important to get an overview of the epistle before analyzing the small parts. Analytical studies begin with Lesson 3.

There are a few basic things to look for in survey study, including first impressions, key words and phrases, structural arrangement of the book, and main emphases. As you begin this "skyscraper view," keep in mind that you are only trying to get an *overall* view of the epistle. This will give you a feel for the book in anticipation of the more detailed studies that follow.

I. MAKING THE FIRST READINGS

A. First Impressions

Scan the epistle once for first impressions. Then answer the following questions.

1. Is this a long epistle?

_____

2. Is it more practical than doctrinal?

_____

3. Are there many personal references?

_____

4. Did you sense any particular tone or atmosphere in the letter?

_____

5. Does Paul seem to have one specific purpose in writing?

_____

6. What are your personal impressions of the book?

_____

_____

B. Paragraph Titles

Read the letter again, a little more slowly. Begin to underline words and phrases that strike you.
1. Make a list of the key words and phrases, and add to the list as you continue your studies.

_____

_____

_____

2. Mark the nineteen paragraph subdivisions in your Bible as shown on Chart B.[1] Then assign a title to each paragraph and record these on the chart. (A paragraph title is a strong word or phrase, taken from the paragraph itself, that is a clue to the general contents of the paragraph. Two examples are shown.)

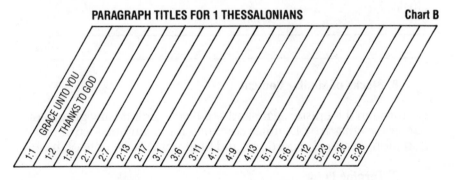

PARAGRAPH TITLES FOR 1 THESSALONIANS   Chart B

C. Main Subjects

Observe the various large subjects referred to by Paul in this epistle. The following list shows some of the more important things that the apostle wanted to include in the letter. As a study exercise, choose one of these subjects and read through the epistle, looking

---

1. Each reference shown on the chart is the first verse of each paragraph.

only for what it says about this particular subject. Extend your study to others of the list, as time permits.

God the Father	Pastoral responsibility
The Lord Jesus	Gospel
(Note the full title "our	Way of salvation
Lord Jesus Christ at 1:3;	Believers
5:9, 23, 28.)	The world
The Holy Spirit	Satan

II. OBSERVING THE STRUCTURE

Each book of the Bible has a structure all its own. (This does not mean that there are no similarities between books. As example of similar pattern is to be found in Paul's epistles, where the early chapters are usually devoted to doctrine and the later chapters to practice.) Let us see how 1 Thessalonians is organized. In doing so, we will get a good perspective of the book's main purposes.

A. Introduction and Conclusion

Read the first paragraphs and the last paragraphs of the epistle. What verses would you identify as the introduction and the conclusion?

_____

_____

B. Blocks of Similar Content

Go through the epistle again and see if you can find any groups of paragraphs that are of similar content—for example, doctrine, exhortation, personal reflections, and biography. Make note of these.

C. Turning Point

Sometimes a book has a turning point, such as a change from doctrine to practice. Do you detect any such change in 1 Thessalonians?

_____

_____

_____

D. High Points and Climax

Occasionally an epistle will reach a high point, or high points, in the course of the writing. A doxology at such a place is often a clue to this. Do you observe any peaks in 1 Thessalonians?

_____

_____

Would you say that there is a definite climax toward the end of the epistle? If so, where, specifically?

_____

E. A Prominent Doctrine

Observe the references to Christ's return at the end of each chapter. What paragraphs in the epistle deal especially with this event of the end times?

_____

_____

III. OUTLINING THE EPISTLE ON A SURVEY CHART

Chart C is a survey chart of 1 Thessalonians, showing the basic structure of the epistle and outlines of various topics. Study this chart carefully. You will want to refer back to it often during the course of your analytical studies, to see the general context of the particular passage you are analyzing.

Observe the following on the chart.

1. The salutation of 1:1 and the assorted verses of 5:23-28 are viewed here as the introduction and conclusion, respectively.

2. A major division appears as 4:1, dividing the epistle into two main parts. What two outlines show this twofold division? Note: the first word of 4:1 in various versions (e.g., Berkeley) is "finally," suggesting a change in Paul's train of thought at this point. Review the survey study made thus far to check whether these twofold outlines represent the epistle's general content.

3. You have already observed that Paul devotes much space to descriptions of his ministry to the Thessalonians. Note the outline, which shows three aspects of that ministry. The segment division shown as 2:17 is based on this observation. Read the paragraphs before and after 2:17 to justify a main division at this point.

Study also the two related outlines that appear just below the _Ministry_ outline.

Chart C

1 THESSALONIANS: THE LORD JESUS IS COMING AGAIN

KEY VERSE:
"I pray God your whole spirit and soul and body be preserved blameless unto the coming of our Lord Jesus Christ" (5:23b).

KEY WORDS:
Lord
brethren (17 times)
sanctification
affliction
coming
gospel
word
day

	LOOKING BACK		LOOKING FORWARD	
	PERSONAL AND HISTORICAL		DIDACTIC AND HORTATORY	—(twofold outline)
				—(threefold outline)
	MINISTRY TO THE THESSALONIANS IN PERSON	MINISTRY IN ABSENTIA	MINISTRY BY EPISTLE	
	WORD AND POWER OF THE SPIRIT	ESTABLISHING AND COMFORTING	CALLING AND CONDUCT · COMFORT (4:13) · SUNDRY COMMANDS (5:12)	
	FAITH	LOVE	HOPE	
	Chap. 1 SALVATION	Chap. 3 SANCTIFICATION	Chap. 4 SORROW · Chap. 5 SOBRIETY	—(fivefold outline) SECOND ADVENT
	EXEMPLARY HOPE of young converts	PURIFYING HOPE of tried believers	COMFORTING HOPE of bereaved saints · INVIGORATING HOPE of diligent Christians	HOPE OF CHRIST'S RETURN
	Chap. 2 SERVICE MOTIVATING HOPE of faithful servants			REFERENCE IN LAST VERSE OF EACH CHAPTER

SALUTATION 1:1 · 1:2
You turned (1:9)
We preached (2:9) · 2:1
We endeavored to see you (2:17) · 2:17
We sent Timothy (3:2)
RE: THESSALONIANS' CONVERSION AND TESTIMONY · RE: PAUL'S SERVICE
FINALLY WE BESEECH 4:1
WE BESEECH 5:1
CONCLUSION 5:23-28

4. One prominent subject of the letter is the Lord's return. It was noted earlier that each chapter ends with a clear reference to this future event. The fivefold topical outlines shown on the survey chart are organized around this observation of the five chapter endings. These outlines also reflect the general content of each of the chapters. For example, the word *salvation* for chapter 1 refers to the Thessalonians' conversion, the experience that accounted for their hope of Christ's return (waiting "for his Son from heaven"—1:10). Study the topical outlines on this theme.

5. Observe on the chart that the title given to the epistle is about the Lord's return. The title is worded this way to anticipate the title of 2 Thessalonians, which is "He Has Not Come Yet." (See Lesson 9.) Note also the key verse.

6. Compare the list of key words with those you have already chosen as key words for 1 Thessalonians.

IV. APPLYING 1 THESSALONIANS TO TODAY

The application of Scripture is universal and timeless. Paul wrote 1 Thessalonians originally to instruct and encourage young converts of Thessalonica in their new Christian experience. That was more than nineteen centuries ago. But God caused this epistle to be included in the New Testament canon so that its message could be profitable for doctrine, reproof, correction, and edification of believers for all the centuries to come. The truths it presents apply not to one age only but to all ages; not to one community only but to the universal church. The same warnings and exhortations that Christians needed in the first century are needed by Christians in this generation.

Beginning with the next lesson, you will analyze each smaller part of 1 Thessalonians. As you study, be alert to any practical lesson—big or small—that you can apply to your own life to help you grow in grace and in the knowledge of Christ, your living Saviour and Lord.

Lesson 3

A Dynamic Local Church

With this lesson we begin our analytical studies of the text of 1 Thessalonians. Analysis is interested in details, down to the smallest unit of a word and even punctuation. In survey study, we made sweeping views of the epistle as a whole. Now we will scrutinize each of the parts, as we keep in mind the whole.

The subject of this lesson is a dynamic local church. The church at Thessalonica was only an infant when Paul wrote this letter, but its fame was widespread because of the miraculous transformation of lives from idolatry to Christianity. Any fellowship of Christians whether it be a local church or lay organization, can learn vital, basic truths about Christian testimony from this short chapter.

CONTEXT OF 1 THESSALONIANS 1   **Chart D**

1:1		4:1	5:28
LOOKING BACK		**LOOKING FORWARD**	
THESSALONIANS' CONVERSION AND TESTIMONY	2:1 PAUL'S SERVICE		

I. PREPARATION FOR STUDY

1. Review your survey study, especially the survey chart. Chart D is an exerpt from the survey chart.

2. Study the map again, observing the key location of Thessalonica. What do the names *Macedonia* and *Achaia* represent?

3. In our survey study, we observed various references in 1 Thessalonians to Christ's second coming. The first of these appears at 1:10. There are different views concerning Christ's second coming. Some hold that His coming will be in two phases; others, that it will be just one event. Chart E shows the premillennial view of two phases, the first called the *rapture*, when Christ will come for His saints, and the second called the *revelation*, when Christ will come with His saints to the earth to set up the millennial kingdom. Chart E shows the sequence of future world events as interpreted by the view of a rapture before the Tribulation. Keep this sequence in mind whenever you study references to Christ's coming.

4. Try to visualize yourself as one of the Christians of Thessalonica, hearing this letter read publicly at the first Sunday service after it arrived at the city. You and your fellow Christians have been saved

PREMILLENNIAL SCHEME OF WORLD EVENTS   **Chart E**

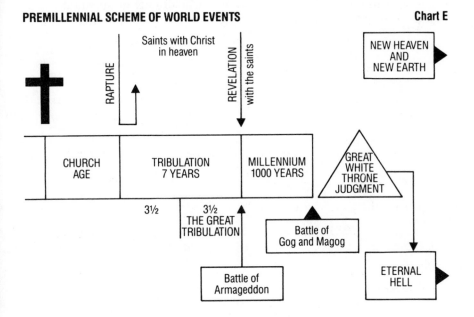

23

only a few months. What would be some of your reactions on hearing Paul's words of chapter 1?

_____

_____

_____

II. ANALYSIS

Segment to be analyzed: 1:1-10
Paragraph divisions: at verses 1, 2, 6

A. General Analysis

1. First, mark the paragraph divisions in your Bible, as identified above. Get in the habit of doing this at the beginning of each analysis. It is important to be paragraph-conscious when studying a segment of the Bible text. (A segment is a group of paragraphs unified by a common theme. The length of a segment may be one full chapter, or shorter, or longer.[1])
2. Read the chapter carefully. Make notations as you go along, such as underlining key words and phrases not already underlined.
3. What is the main point of each paragraph? Record them.
1:1

_____

1:2-5

_____

1:6-10

_____

4. Whom does Paul write more about here, himself or the Thessalonians?

_____

5. What is the tone of the passage?

_____

6. How are the three Persons of the Trinity referred to in the segment?

_____

1. Actually the introductory salutation is a unit by itself, apart from the segment 1:2-10. We will study all ten verses as one segment.

What works are ascribed to each?

_____

_____

_____

7. Does the chapter end on a climactic note? If so, what is it?

_____

B. Paragraph Analysis

1. *Paragraph 1:1*: Salutation
Compare the salutations of a few of Paul's other epistles. Do you observe any pattern? What quality do you see in Paul by his inclusion of the names of two co-workers in the salutation?

_____

How does Paul identify the church of the Thessalonians?

_____

What does the small word "in" suggest, spiritually speaking? Compare Colossians 3:3.

_____

_____

The phrase "God the Father, and the Lord Jesus Christ" is repeated, essentially, in the next paragraph. Why the repetition?

_____

_____

Note that the relationship to "God the Father" identifies the Thessalonians as nonheathen, whereas that to "Lord Jesus Christ" marks them as non-Israelite.

    Ponder the full teaching of the threefold designation "Lord Jesus Christ," in view of these meanings:

    (a) "Lord" —master (cf. John 20:28)

    (b) "Jesus" —Savior (cf. Matt. 1:21)

    (c) "Christ" —the anointed one, or Messiah (cf. John 1:41)

2. *Paragraph 1:2-5*: Thanks to God
What ministries of Paul are cited in this paragraph?

1:2 _____

1:3*a* _____

1:5 _____

What do verses 2 and 3*a* teach about gratitude to God and about prayer?

_____

_____

_____

Observe the triad of faith, love, and hope in 1:3.[2] With what is each virtue identified in the verse?

(a) faith _____

(b) love _____

(c) hope _____
Do you see any references to these in the last paragraph? Is there a logical and chronological order in this triad? (Compare the order of faith, hope, and love in 1 Cor. 13:13.) Recall the outline of faith, love, and hope on the survey Chart C. What three strong words in verse 4 identify the Thessalonian Christians?

_____

_____

Observe how the beautiful truths of each word are woven together in this expanded paraphrase of the verse.

> You are our brothers,
> on whom God has set His love;
> we recognize you full well as those whom He has chosen.[3]

On the meaning of "election," see Ephesians 1:4-5.
    What descriptions does Paul give in verse 5 concerning how he ministered the gospel to the Thessalonians? Record each phrase.

in _____

in _____

in _____

in _____

2. This is the earliest appearance of Paul's famous group of graces, known to most people in the more familiar passage of 1 Corinthians 13:13. Compare also Colossians 1:4-5 and 1 Thessalonians 5:8.
3. *Expanded Paraphrase*, by F. F. Bruce. This paraphrase correctly brings "beloved" and "of God" (King James Version) together.

What does the last phrase ("as ye know") add to the above description?

_____

_____

3. *Paragraph 1:6-10*: Ensamples to All
Compare these three phrases:
    (a) "followers of us" (1:6)
    (b) "followers of the Lord" (1:6)
    (c) "ensamples to all" (1:7)
(See Notes on the words "followers" and "ensamples.") Note the combination "in much affliction, with joy" (1:6). What is Paul's brief explanation of such a seeming contradiction?

_____

_____

What is the main point of 1:7-9*a*?

_____

_____

How is geography involved in broadcast in this instance?

_____

_____

Analyze carefully verses 9 and 10. Observe the time references. What phrase do you relate to each of the following?

(a) past: "ye _____"

(b) present: "to _____"

(c) future (prospect): "to _____"
What does 1:9 reveal about the Thessalonians' previous religious life?

_____

_____

What is the strength of the words "living and true" in describing God?

_____

_____

How does verse 10 authenticate such a description?

_____

What three events does Paul cite in verse 10? Which still await fulfillment? Locate these on Chart E.

_____

_____

What does 1:10 teach about man's need of salvation?

_____

What other truths about salvation does the entire passage teach?

_____

_____

_____

III. NOTES

1. *"Grace be unto you, and peace"* (1:1). In early Greek correspondence, the common salutation was "greetings" ("rejoice"—cf. James 1:1). Jews usually used the word "peace" (*shalom*). The salutation used mostly in the New Testament epistles, "grace and peace," has the flavor of the gospel in it, for grace is God's unmerited favor to man, and peace comes to all who receive that favor in Christ.

2. *"Election"* (1:4). This redemptive election of saints by God has been defined as "that sovereign act of God in grace whereby He chose in Christ Jesus for salvation all those whom He foreknew would accept Him."[4] See Romans 8:29-20.

3. *"Followers"* (1:6). The Greek word is better translated "imitators." The same word appears in the following verses: 1 Corinthians 4:16; 11:1; Ephesians 5:1; 1 Thessalonians 2:14; Hebrews 6:12.

4. *"Ensamples"* (1:7). The original word means literally a type, a mold, or a pattern. It is used with this meaning in these verses: Philippians 3:17; 2 Thessalonians 3:9; 1 Timothy 4:12; 1 Peter 5:3.

5. *"In every place your faith . . . is spread abroad"* (1:8). Paul had just arrived at Corinth, where he met Aquila and Priscilla, who

4. Henry Clarence Thiessen, *Introductory Lectures in Systematic Theology*, p. 344.

had recently come from Italy. (See Acts 18:1-2.) It is possible that Aquila and Priscilla told Paul that news about the Thessalonian church had reached even as far as Rome.

IV. FOR THOUGHT AND DISCUSSION

1. How can Christians experience joy in the midst of affliction (1:6)? See John 16:33; Acts 16:23-25; Galatians 5:22; Hebrews 12:2; 1 Peter 1:3-9; 2:19-21.
2. What is the best testimony a Christian can bear to unsaved people?
3. Why is it important for Christians to be good examples to other Christians? (1:7)
4. How sure are you that Jesus will return to this earth? What is the basis of your assurance? Read Isaiah 14:24.
5. What characteristics of a spiritually vibrant local church have you observed in the passage of this lesson?
6. Paul wrote that the Thessalonian Christians had turned to God to serve Him (1:9). Believers are bondslaves of God and of Christ. What does this suggest to you concerning Christian service?
7. What did Paul mean when he wrote, "Ye became imitators [followers, KJV*] of us, and of the Lord" (1:6)? Was the apostle presuming too much?

V. FURTHER STUDY

Whenever necessary, use outside helps to complete studies suggested in this section of each lesson. Such helps include an exhaustive concordance, a topical or word study book, a book on Bible doctrines, and a Bible dictionary.

Subjects suggested for further study
1. The New Testament teaching on the local church and the church universal (Body of Christ).
2. The coming wrath of God. Some verses to consult are Romans 3:5; 5:9; Revelation 19:11-21.

VI. WORDS TO PONDER

You **turned** to God from idols to serve a living and true God; and to **wait for** His Son from heaven (1:9b-10a).

---

*King James Version.

29

A Successful Christian Worker

The enemies of Paul had driven him from Thessalonica with the hope of aborting his evangelistic mission. Luke records some of this physical opposition in Acts 17:5-15. Apparently the enemies pursued with other tactics as well, such as slanderous rumors about Paul's personal life, motives, and methods in his gospel campaigns. This would account for Paul's devoting so much space in this short epistle to defending his ministry. Just what the apostle said about himself is the main subject of this lesson's passage. Here is a true picture of a successful Christian worker, accomplishing God's will against all human odds. You will be able to

CONTEXT OF 1 THESSALONIANS 2:1-16   **Chart F**

1:1	2:1	2:17	4:1	5:28
	LOOKING BACK		LOOKING FORWARD	
	PERSONAL AND HISTORICAL		DIDACTIC AND HORTATORY	
Paul's ministry in person		Paul's ministry in absentia	Paul's ministry by epistle	
mainly about the Thessalonians	mainly about Paul			

THIS LESSON

30

learn many valuable lessons as you study the warm testimony of this man of God.

I. PREPARATION FOR STUDY

1. Read Acts 17:1-15, observing especially the opposition to Paul's ministry at Thessalonica.

2. Also read Acts 16:12-40, noting the opposition Paul encountered at Philippi. Paul refers to this in 1 Thessalonians 2:2.

3. Keep in mind where the present passage appears in the overall pattern of the epistle. Chart F shows this context.

II. ANALYSIS

Segment to be analyzed: 2:1-16
Paragraph divisions: at verses 1, 7, 13

A. General Analysis

1. Observe on Chart G that most of 2:1-16 is about Paul. How does this compare with chapter 1? Read 2:1-16. Which paragraphs are about Paul, and which one says more about the Thessalonians?

2. Read the segment again, paragraph by paragraph. What is the main theme of each paragraph? (Use the worksheet of Chart G to record this and other observations.) The following clues will help you see the overall differences between the paragraphs.

(a) Note Paul's *negative* approach in paragraph 2:1-6. Underline every negative word (such as *nor*).

(b) Contrast the above with the positive, constructive things Paul says in paragraph 2:7-12. Underline the various constructive ministries of Paul in behalf of the Thessalonians.

(c) Was the emphasis in the first two paragraphs on Paul's *outgoing* ministry? Compare this with the *response* of the Thessalonians, as described in the third paragraph (2:13-16). The key clue word here is "received" (2:13).

3. Observe the main topical study of the analytical Chart G. The key center, chosen arbitrarily, is *the gospel of God.*[1] Note the paragraph points related to this title as they appear in the lefthand margin. Try making a similar outline of your own, choosing a key

---

1. The key center of an analytical chart may be any key word or phrase that is seen to relate to a truth in each paragraph of the segment. Since there are many such words or phrases in any particular segment, the choice of *the gospel of God* is identified here as an arbitrary one.

31

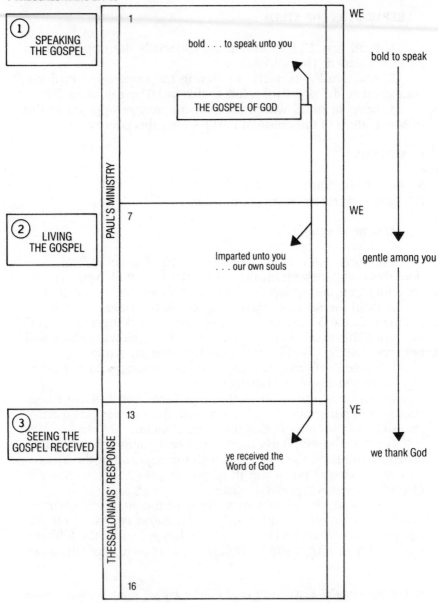

SPEAKING
THE GOSPEL

LIVING
THE GOSPEL

SEEING THE
GOSPEL RECEIVED

PAUL'S MINISTRY

THESSALONIANS' RESPONSE

THE GOSPEL OF GOD

bold . . . to speak unto you

Imparted unto you
. . . our own souls

ye received the
Word of God

WE

WE

YE

bold to speak

gentle among you

we thank God

center from any of the paragraphs and arriving at a master title and paragraph points from it.

4. What is the overall tone of this passage? If slanderous rumors had been circulating about Paul, does he show any signs of bitterness, anger, or vengeance?

B. Paragraph Analysis

1. *Paragraph 2:1-6*: Speaking the Gospel
What different references are made to God? List them.

_____

_____

_____

_____

_____

Make a list of all the things Paul says he did not do in his mission of preaching the gospel to the Thessalonians. What rumor may he have been answering in each case?

_____

_____

_____

_____

Paul refers to himself as an apostle of Christ (2:6). (Cf. 1 Cor. 9:1-2.) Relate this to other phrases in the paragraph, such as "in trust with the gospel" (2:4). (On the latter phrase, compare 1 Cor. 9:17; Gal. 2:7; 1 Tim. 1:11; Titus 1:3.)

2. *Paragraph 2:7-12*: Living the Gospel
Note the key opening word of the paragraph (2:7). What does it indicate?

_____

_____

What twofold ministry did Paul share with the Thessalonians, as indicated by 2:8? Which of the two is this paragraph mainly about?

_____

_____

_____

List the commendable things Paul claims for his ministry to the Thessalonians.

_____

_____

_____

_____

_____

Observe the metaphors of nurse (2:7) and father (2:11). How does Paul apply each of these?
a. *Nurse* and children:

_____

_____

b. *Father* and children:

_____

_____

What kind of work is Paul referring to in 2:9? (See Acts 18:3; 20:34; 2 Thess. 3:7-12.) How do you reconcile this with the principle of Luke 10:7 and 1 Timothy 5:18?

_____

_____

What tender phrases appear in this paragraph?

_____

_____

What does this reveal about Paul?

_____

_____

What threefold ministry is mentioned in 2:11?

_____

_____

3. *Paragraph 2:13-16*: Seeing the Gospel Received
Note the key word "received" in verse 13. What was Paul's cause for thanksgiving?

_____

_____

What is boldly contrasted in verse 13? Compare Galatians 1:11-12.

_____

_____

Analyze the last part of verse 13: "which effectually worketh also in you that believe." What does this add to what Paul had already written in the verse about the Thessalonians' receiving the Word? (Cf. Rom. 1:16; Heb. 4:12; James 1:21; 1 Peter 1:23.)

_____

_____

How would the message of 2:14-16 be an encouragement to the persecuted saints at Thessalonica?

_____

_____

In what three ways are the local churches of 2:14 identified?

_____

_____

_____

What are the various indictments of 2:15-16?

_____

_____

Compare the readings of other versions beginning at the phrase "to fill up" (2:16). Here is the paraphrase of _The Living Bible_: "And so their sins continue to grow. But the anger of God has caught up with them at last." This is the second of three appearances of the word "wrath" in the epistle. Compare the reference here with that of 1:10 and 5:9. To summarize: what commendations does Paul have for the Thessalonians?

_____

_____

_____

III. NOTES

1. _"Contention"_ (2:2). In everyday life, the Greek word was used to describe the rigors of the athletic contests in the sports arenas. The same word is translated "conflict" in Philippians 1:30 and Colossians 2:1.

2. *"Allowed of God"* (2:4). The word "allowed" means approved as the outcome of the proving (cf. 1 Peter 1:7). Bruce's *Expanded Paraphrase* reads, "Our accreditation came from God Himself." Paul's period of probation from the time of his conversion (Acts 9) to the beginning of a gospel ministry at Antioch (Acts 11:25-26) lasted about ten years. This man of zeal and fervor must have learned much patience and perseverance in this long interim.

3. *"Nurse"* (2:7). This is correctly read as "nursing mother," which is the word's intention.

4. *"Cherisheth"* (2:7). The word means literally "to warm." Compare Ephesians 5:29, where it is used of Christ and the church.

5. *"Laboring night and day"* (2:9). It is possible that Paul arose before dawn and tarried after dusk to work on tentmaking so that he would have long days of spiritual ministry among the people. He made his living by tentmaking in order to leave no room for misunderstanding concerning his financial support. One commentator suggests that some of Paul's opponents were unbelieving husbands of the rich ladies who had become members of the church (Acts 17:4).

6. *"Worthy of God"* (2:12). This should read "worthily of God."

7. *"Kingdom"* (2:12). The New Testament refers to a present kingdom (cf. Rom. 14:17; 1 Cor. 4:20; Col. 1:13) and a future kingdom (cf. Matt. 25:34; Acts 14:22; 1 Cor. 6:9; 15:50; Gal. 5:21). Because Paul associates "kingdom" with "glory" in 2:12, we conclude that he is thinking here of the future kingdom of God. "By faith they [the Thessalonian Christians] had already entered the kingdom of God, but the revelation of its full glory belonged to a day yet future; they were, however, heirs of that glory, and must live accordingly."[2]

8. *"Received"* (2:13). Two different Greek words are translated "received" in this verse. The word appearing first means the outward hearing by the ear; the second word means the inward reception by the heart. (Cf. Matt. 13:13.)

9. *"Your own countrymen"* (2:14). From the Acts account (17:5), we may gather that both Jews and Gentiles are meant by this designation.

10. *"Wrath is come upon them to the uttermost"* (2:16). Read Deuteronomy 28:15-68 for a prophecy of judgment upon Israel for rejecting God and His Word. When Paul wrote 1 Thessaloni-

---

2. F. F. Bruce, "The Epistles to the Thessalonians," in *The New Bible Commentary*, ed. F. Davidson, A. M. Stibbs, and E. F. Kevan, p. 1055.

ans, the judgments obviously had not fully come, though the Jews were already a scattered people and their land was under foreign yoke. Vincent interprets this phrase thus: "The wrath of God had *not* come upon them to the uttermost [to the end]. The meaning is that the divine wrath had reached the point where it passed into judgment."

IV. FOR THOUGHT AND DISCUSSION

1. What are the traits of a good apostle of Christ, as taught by this passage?

2. Are any preachers today guilty of preaching the word of men rather than the Word of God (2:13)? If so, what are some of the causes? What is the solution?

3. The phrase "gospel of God" appears twice in this passage. What does the phrase mean to you?

4. What must a Christian do to "walk worthily of God" (2:12)?

5. It is God who calls men and women into His kingdom. What are some practical, spiritual lessons suggested by this awesome and wonderful truth?

6. The word *saved* (2:16) is often spoken lightly, without serious thought of its implications. What do you think of when you speak of yourself or another as being saved?

V. FURTHER STUDY

Study what the New Testament teaches about the financial support of Christian workers such as pastors and missionaries. Include in your study the following passages: 1 Corinthians 9:1-15; 2 Corinthians 11:7-12; Galatians 6:6; 2 Thessalonians 3:7-12.

VI. WORDS TO PONDER

We encouraged you, we comforted you, and we kept urging you to live the kind of life that pleases God (2:12, *Today's English Version*).

3. Marvin R. Vincent, *Word Studies in the New Testament*, 4:29.

Ministering to Christians in Absentia

One of the great spiritual qualities of Paul was that he was always thinking of the needs of others. In the passage of our present lesson, he regrets that he cannot be with the Thessalonian Christians in person for the time being. But this separation does not relieve his responsibility as the Thessalonians' spiritual shepherd and father. He does two definite things on their behalf. He sends Timothy to minister to them in his place, and he intercedes for them night and day before the throne of God. We might call this a ministry by proxy and by prayer. Ministering to others in absentia can be as fruitful as a ministry in person. Do you know of someone living hundreds of miles from you for whom you could perform a spiritual ministry today?

I. PREPARATION FOR STUDY

1. Review the story in Acts that tells how Paul was separated from the Thessalonians in the first place (Acts 17:5-10). Since Paul's escape from Thessalonica was so swift and secret, do you think there may have been some unfinished business left there as a consequence?

Read also Acts 17:15-16, which reports Paul's arrival at Athens (see 1 Thess. 3:1); and Acts 18:1, which reports his arrival at Corinth, from which he wrote the Thessalonian letters.

2. The passage of this lesson is the second of three divisions of the epistle concerning Paul's ministry to the church at Thessalonica. This is shown on Chart H. Compare this with the survey of Chart C.

3. The word "coming," in such phrases as "the coming of our Lord," first appears in the segment that we shall be studying in this

1:1	2:17 3:13	4:1 5:28
ministry to the Thessalonians in person	ministry to the Thessalonians in absentia	ministry to the Thessalonians by epistle
▼	▼	▼
BY WORD AND POWER	BY PROXY AND PRAYER	BY EXHORTATION AND COMMAND
faith	love	hope

lesson.[1] It would be helpful to pause at this point and consider the meaning and significance of the word. Study carefully the following notes.

(a) The word "coming" in 2:19 and 3:13 translates the Greek word *parousia*. The word means literally "presence" (*para*, with, plus *ousia*, being). The opposite word is *apousia*, translated "absence." Paul uses both words in an interesting way in Philippians 2:12, "not as in my presence (*parousia*) only, but now much more in my absence (*apousia*)."

(b) The word *parousia* really has a double meaning: an arrival, and a presence. One can see how the word was used in both ways, since there can be no presence without arrival. In most of the New Testament eschatological (last times) references, the emphasis is on the *arrival* of Christ.[2] (Perhaps the word *visit* would better translate *parousia*, since it includes both ideas.)

(c) *Parousia* always refers to a period of time, more or less extended.[3] When used prophetically of Christ, it refers to a period

---

1. Appearances of the word in the Thessalonian epistles: 1 Thessalonians 2:19; 3:13; 4:15; 5:23; 2 Thessalonians 2:1, 8-9. (The last reference is to the Antichrist.)
2. Here is an example of how the word came to be used in the Hellenistic vernacular of Paul's day: "of the arrival of some dignitary to pay an official visit to a place" (F. F. Bruce. "The Epistles to the Thessalonians," in *The New Bible Commentary*, p. 1055).
3. C. F. Hogg and W. E. Vine, *The Thessalonian Epistles*, p. 87.

that shall begin with Christ's descent from heaven to rapture the saints. Read 1 Thessalonians 4:15-16.

(d) In some prophetic passages of the New Testament, the word gives prominence to the beginning (event of arrival) of Christ's *parousia*. Read 1 Corinthians 15:23; 1 Thessalonians 4:15; 5:23; 2 Thessalonians 2:1; James 5:7-8; 2 Peter 3:4.

(e) In some passages, *parousia* emphasizes the course of the period. Read 1 Thessalonians 3:13; 1 John 2:28.

(f) Some passages give prominence to the conclusion of the *parousia*. Read Matthew 24:27; 2 Thessalonians 2:8.

(g) Relate all of the above discussion to Chart E, as concerns the two phases of Christ's second coming, namely, the rapture and the revelation.

(h) Whenever you read the word "coming" in the Thessalonian letters, consider the root idea of "presence" when making your interpretations. (See the marginal notes of the *New American Standard Bible* at 1 Thess. 2:19; 3:13.)

4. As you analyze 2:17–3:13, keep in mind that the goal of your Bible study is to apply the Scriptures to everyday living. Watch especially how Paul ministered in absentia to the needs of those whom he had recently led to the Lord.

II. ANALYSIS

Segment to be analyzed: 2:17–3:13
Paragraph divisions: at verses 2:17; 3:1, 6, 11

A. General Analysis

1. Chart I is a partially completed analytical chart, which you may use to record further observations of the text as you proceed with your analysis.

2. It was noted earlier in this lesson that 2:17–3:13 is about Paul's ministry to the Thessalonians while he was separated from them. (Hence a new segment is made to begin at 2:17 instead of at 3:1.) Scan the four paragraphs of the segment and observe at least one phrase in each paragraph that indicates this kind of distant ministry. Complete the outline shown in the righthand margin of Chart I, beginning with "taken from you" (2:17).

3. Read the segment in your Bible, paragraph by paragraph. What is Paul's main point in each paragraph?

4. Observe on Chart I that the first and last paragraphs are set off from the middle two. Study the outlines in the two narrow vertical columns to see the reason for this. Justify the outlines from the content of the paragraphs in the Bible text. Note the contrasts

40

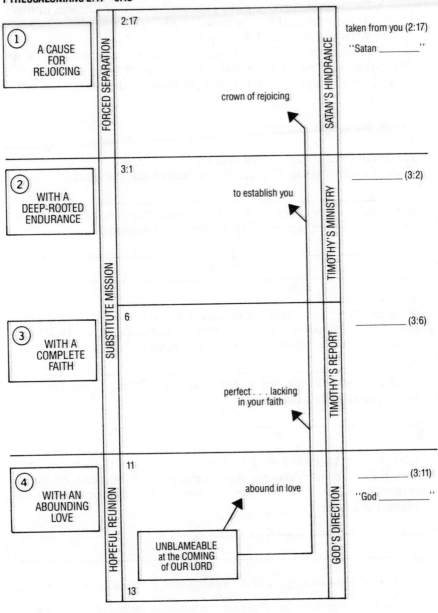

of the first and last paragraphs. Why is a new paragraph made at verse 6?

5. Did you observe any key repeated words or phrases in this segment? How often does the word "faith" appear?

6. What is the tone of this segment?

7. How does the last paragraph serve as a conclusion to the first three chapters of 1 Thessalonians?[4] (Recall from your survey study that 4:1 begins an entirely new thought in the epistle. See Chart C.)

B. Paragraph Analysis

1. *Paragraph 2:17-20*: Glory and Joy
What phrase of verse 17 gives the setting of this paragraph?

_____

What different phrases of 2:17-18 indicate the intensity of Paul's feelings on being separated from the Thessalonians?

_____

_____

What are ways in which Satan may have hindered Paul from returning to Thessalonica at this time? (Compare Rom. 15:20-22, which refers to a hindrance of another kind.)

_____

What contrasts do you see in this paragraph between the last two verses and the first two verses?

_____

Why did Paul include 2:19-20 at this point? Do you think Satan hindered him from revisiting the Thessalonians because of their common hope of future victory, symbolized by the crown to which Paul refers?[5]

_____

_____

4. Some ancient manuscripts add the word "Amen" at the end of 3:13 (see *Amplified Bible*).
5. This crown is perhaps "an allusion to the wreath or garland of victory awarded to winners in the games or to distinguished public servants" (D. A. Hubbard, "The First Epistle to the Thessalonians," in *The Wycliffe Bible Commentary*, p. 1,352).

2. *Paragraph 3:1-5*: Suffering to Come

In what three ways does Paul identify Timothy in 3:2? What is meant in each case?

_____

_____

_____

What various ministries was Timothy sent to accomplish? (3:2-5)

_____

_____

What was Paul's concern? (3:3-5)

_____

_____

How is the devil identified in 3:5? Compare this with the name *Satan* (see *Notes*).

_____

_____

What sobering fact is suggested by the phrase "lest . . . our labor be in vain" (3:5)?

_____

_____

Why did Paul place such a premium on *faith* in the Thessalonians' Christian walk?

_____

_____

3. *Paragraph 3:6-10*: Stability in the Faith

What phrase of 3:6 provides the setting of this paragraph?

_____

What is the tone of the paragraph? Compare it with that of the previous paragraph.

_____

_____

What was Timothy's report about the Thessalonians' faith? (3:6-7, 10)

_____

What is Paul really saying in verse 8? Compare various modern versions.

_____

_____

_____

What two prayer requests does Paul cite in 3:10?

_____

_____

What does he mean by the phrase "that we . . . might perfect that which is lacking in your faith" (3:10)?

_____

_____

4. *Paragraph 3:11-13*: Prayer for Sanctification
What is the apostle's wish as expressed in 3:11?

_____

What is the key word of Paul's wish of 3:12?

_____

What is the strength of the words "increase" and "abound" (3:12)?

_____

_____

Make a list of the various truths taught by 3:13. Include the following:
(a) Purpose of the divine work described in the previous verse

_____

(b) Ultimate condition of the believer's heart

_____

(c) Relationships

"your hearts . . . before _____"

"Lord Jesus Christ with _____"

Note the phrase of 3:13: "stablish your hearts unblameable in holiness." The word "stablish" is the same as "establish" of 3:3. The highest spiritual attainment of any Christian is to be "unblameable in holiness," but this will not take place until the time of Christ's coming (3:13*b*). So while we await His coming, God seeks to do a continuing work of establishing, or confirming, our hearts in faith.

Note the main topical study shown on Chart I centered on the title "Unblameable at Christ's Coming." Relate each of the four phrases of the lefthand column to this title. Is it true that our present daily living is closely related to the event of Christ's return? (Read 1 John 2:28; 3:1-3 for light on this.) What picture do you get from the last phrase of 3:13: "at the coming of our Lord Jesus Christ with all his saints"?

_____

_____

_____

III. NOTES

1. *"In presence"* (2:17). The word is not *parousia*, discussed earlier in this lesson. A literal translation is "in face," the word appearing again toward the end of the verse. A natural and accurate translation is "in person" (*New American Standard Bible*).

2. *"Satan hindered us"* (2:18). The name "Satan" means, literally, "adversary." Paul does not indicate how Satan hindered him. Various obstacles have been suggested:

(a) illness (cf. 2 Cor. 12:7; Gal. 4:13)

(b) opposition in Athens detaining him there (cf. 1 Thess. 3:1)

(c) the exacting of bond from Jason to insure that Paul would not return to Thessalonica (Acts 17:9)

Paul was a realist concerning the power of Satan and his antagonism against all Christians as permitted by the omnipotent and sovereign Saviour of those very Christians.

3. *"In the presence of"* (2:19). The root of the word so translated is the same as that translated "in presence" in verse 17.

4. *"Perfect"* (3:10). This is a common New Testament term, mistakenly interpreted by some as "sinless" or "flawless." The term means "to fit a thing for its full and proper use, supplying what is needed." The idea of making sinless or flawless is not in the term.

5. *"That which is lacking in your faith"* (3:10). This is not a reference to the Thessalonians' faith that saved them. Rather it is a reference to the exercise of their faith in everyday conduct, in their understanding of various doctrines of truth (such as the Lord's second coming) and in their mutual relationships in the ministry of the church. These are some of the reasons for the instructions and exhortations of the remainder of the epistle.

6. *"Abound in love"* (3:12). This is Christlike *agape,* a selfless giving of oneself to others without expecting a return. Hogg and Vine give this partial description:

> Christian love, whether exercised toward the brethren, or toward men generally, is not an impulse from the feelings, it does not always run with the natural inclinations, nor does it spend itself only upon those for whom some affinity is discovered. Love seeks the welfare of all, Rom. 15:2, and works no ill to any, 13:8-10; love seeks opportunity to do good to "all men, and especially toward them that are of the household of the faith," Gal. 6:10.[6]

7. *"Saints"* (3:13). The word literally means "holy ones" and here refers to the spirits of deceased believers (see 4:14). In this verse, it may refer also to holy angels who will attend Christ's coming. (Cf. Matt. 25:31; Mark 8:38.)

IV. FOR THOUGHT AND DISCUSSION

1. Paul had won the Thessalonian converts to the Lord, so he viewed them as one of his crowns in heaven (2:19).[7] Do you think any others (e.g., Timothy) would share in that reward? If so, on what basis?

2. How does a Christian's faith grow and mature? What are some hindrances to such growth?

3. According to the Bible, afflictions and trials are part of the Christian's experience. (Read John 15:20; 16:33; Acts 14:22; Rom. 5:3.) If you are studying in a group, discuss the following commentary:

> It is taken for granted throughout the New Testament that affliction is the normal lot of Christians; it is, in fact, an evidence of the genuineness of their faith and an earnest of their part in the coming glory. Cf. Acts xiv. 22; Rom. vii. 17f.; 2 Tim. ii. 12. . . . What had been an acute problem to faith in Old Testament times—the suffering of the righteous—had come to be recognized as an essential element in God's purpose for His people. Since their Lord Himself had suffered, they need expect nothing else.[8]

---

6. C. F. Hogg and W. E. Vine, *The Thessalonian Epistles*, pp. 105-6.
7. The pronouns "we," "us," and "our" in these verses are editorial pronouns, intending only the writer, Paul.
8. Bruce, p. 1,055.

4. How can Christians prove their love toward each other and toward unsaved people (3:12; cf. Gal. 6:10; 2 Pet. 1:7)? Do you think it was easy for the Thessalonian Christians to keep their hearts pure from any taint of bitterness and vengeance against their fellow countrymen who had treated Paul so cruelly before their very eyes?

5. What important spiritual lessons are taught by this passage?

V. FURTHER STUDY

1. Study the subject of Christ's return. Arrive at your own conclusions as to whether Christ's second coming will be in one phase, or two; and if the latter, how long will be the period between the two phases (rapture, revelation). Do you think the last phrase of 3:13 refers to Christ's coming of 4:14-15 or of Revelation 19:11-14?

2. It is always sobering to reflect on the herculean powers that God has permitted Satan to exercise. Read Job 1:6-12; Zechariah 3:1; 2 Corinthians 4:4; Ephesians 2:2; 6:12; and 1 Peter 5:8-9. What do you think is God's reason for allowing such opposition?

3. Make a word study in the New Testament of the word *perfect*, as it is used in various ways. Include in your study the following verses.[9] Record the King James translation, and what appears to be the intended meaning, in line with the context.

Table 2

Verse	King James Translation	Meaning
Matthew 4:21	''mending''	restoring back to the original state
Galatians 6:1	''restore''	
Hebrews 11:3	''framed''	
Matthew 21:16		
Hebrews 13:21		
1 Peter 5:10		

VI. WORDS TO PONDER

The Lord enable you more and more
to spend your lives in the interests of others,
in order that He may so establish you

9. In each verse cited, the same Greek word *katartizo* appears. Strong's *Exhaustive Concordance* or Young's *Analytical Concordance* supplies this information.

in Christian character now, that you may
be vindicated from every charge that
might possibly be brought against you at the
Judgment-seat of God
    (3:13, paraphrase by Hogg and Vine)

Lesson 6

The Life That Pleases God

A t this point in his epistle Paul begins to exhort the Thessalonians concerning their daily behavior. Paul never wrote a letter without appealing for Christian conduct that magnified Christ and pleased God. The apostle here reminds the Thessalonians that he had earlier instructed them about these things when he was with them. Now, he writes, "keep on" living in that way, but "doing still better" (4:1, Berkeley). Healthy Christian living is not static; it is always dynamic. Christians are to keep growing, moving, abounding. As someone has said, "There is no finality in practical holiness while the Christian remains on the earth."

I. PREPARATION FOR STUDY

1. Reread the last paragraph of chapter 3, recalling from your study of last lesson how that paragraph concluded the first large section of the epistle (1:1–3:13). Then read the first word of 4:1 as "finally," as it is translated in some versions (e.g., NASB). As we observed in our survey study of 1 Thessalonians, 4:1 is the beginning of the practical section of the epistle.
2. Chart J shows the context of the passage of our present lesson. Keep this in mind as you study 4:1-12.
3. Consult a dictionary for present-day meanings of the following words that appear in this passage:
(a) sanctification (4:3-4)

_____

(b) fornication (4:3)

_____

(c) concupiscence (4:5)

_____

1:1		4:1		5:28
PERSONAL AND HISTORICAL		**DIDACTIC AND HORTATORY**		
	2:17			
Paul's ministry in person	Paul's ministry in absentia	Paul's ministry by epistle		
		CALLING AND CONDUCT	4:13 COMFORT	5:12 SUNDRY COMMANDS

THIS LESSON

4. The doctrine of sanctification in the Bible is an important one. The root of the term is a word meaning "holy," which in its absolute form is a primary attribute of God. This raises a practical question, "How can a human being be made holy (that is, be sanctified)?" Answers to this question are suggested by the following.

(a) Sanctification is both separation *from* evil and consecration *unto* righteousness.

(b) Sometimes the word *sanctification* (or its synonym *holiness*) in the Bible is used positionally, that is, God sees the Christian as holy because He sees him in Christ. (Cf. 1 Cor. 1:30; Heb. 10:14.)

(c) Sometimes the word is used experientially, when referring to the ever-progressing growth of the Christian in righteousness (e.g., 1 Thess. 4:7; Heb. 12:14). Complete holiness (sinless perfection) is not reached in this life.

(d) Sometimes the doctrine of sanctification appears in the Bible as referring to the ultimate and complete work of God, when He glorifies the believer in the sinless state at the coming of Christ (cf. 1 John 3:2). This is how the word *holiness* is used in 1 Thessalonians 3:13, studied earlier.

Refer to the above discussion when you study the words *holiness* and *sanctification* in the present passage.

5. It would take a lengthy book for a New Testament author to write about all aspects of Christian conduct. The writers of the

50

epistles did not intend to include everything in their letters to churches and individuals. Instead they were inspired to choose those things that pertained to that particular situation. If Paul wrote about a particular sin in such a short letter as 1 Thessalonians, do you think that sin was, or threatened to be, a problem in the church at that time? You will want to bear this in mind as you study 4:1-12.

II. ANALYSIS

Segment to be analyzed: 4:1-12
Paragraph divisions: at verses 1, 9

A. General Analysis

1. Read the segment through once. What is Paul's method of approach in appealing for response?

_____

_____

What different phrases in the segment refer to instruction given to the Thessalonians? Record them.

_____

_____

_____

_____

2. What is the main point of each paragraph?
4:1-8:

_____

4:9-12:

_____

3. Compare the phrases:
    (a) "abound more and more" (4:1)
    (b) "increase more and more" (4:10)
How do these phrases indicate Paul's purpose in writing this practical passage to the Thessalonians?

_____

_____

_____

B. Paragraph Analysis

1. *Paragraph 4:1-8*: Life of Purity
How do the first two verses serve to introduce this entire last section of the epistle (4:1–5:28)?

_____

_____

_____

Account for the repeated thought in the two words "beseech" and "exhort" (4:1).

_____

_____

_____

What spiritual truths are suggested by the two picture words "walk" and "please" (4:1)?

_____

_____

Paul had given the Thessalonians some "commandments . . . by the Lord Jesus" (4:2). Do you think these were in Paul's words or in Jesus' words?

_____

Have you ever asked the question, How can I know the will of God? Observe that one aspect of the will of God is stated explicitly in verse 3.
What is it?

_____

Is this a major aspect?

_____

_____

What kind of sin does Paul refer to consistently, beginning at 4:3?

_____

It has been observed by one writer that "no temptation faced by the early church was more vexing than that of immorality."[1]
List the negative and positive appeals of this paragraph.

1. David A. Hubbard, "The First Epistle to the Thessalonians," in *The Wycliffe Bible Commentary*, p. 1353.

52

Negative	Positive

See *Notes* on the phrases "possess his vessel" (4:4) and "defraud his brother" (4:6).

Observe a different reference to God in each of the last three verses (6, 7, 8). What is the reference, and how does each one support and strengthen Paul's command about holy living?

4:6

_____

4:7

_____

4:8

_____

Relate the word "holiness" of 4:7 to the word "holy" of 4:8.

2. *Paragraph 4:9-12*: Life of Brotherly Love

The familiar word *philadelphia* is the Greek word translated "brotherly love" in 4:9. (See *Notes*.) What does Paul write about this in verses 9 and 10?

_____

_____

Relate Paul's commendation "ye do it" to the exhortation "increase" (4:10).

_____

Do the commands of verses 11 and 12 have anything to do with the appeal for brotherly love? If so, what is the connection?

_____

_____

List the different commands of 4:11-12. Concerning the command about working: since the Thessalonians were thinking much about the Lord's imminent return, do you think some of them may have been neglecting their work in the meantime? (Cf. 2 Thess. 3:11.)

III. NOTES

1. *"Abstain from fornication"* (4:3). Paul wrote this to all the saints at Thessalonica, not because all were fornicators but because this was a strong temptation for many of the Thessalonian believers. "Fornication was widely regarded in the Graeco-Roman world as almost on the same level of ethical indifference as food and drink."[2] Christians recently converted from the paganism of such a culture were sorely vexed by the temptation to such immorality. This accounts for the inclusion of a prohibition against fornication in the decree of the Jerusalem Council (Acts 15:29), a decree addressed to Christians.

2. *"Possess his vessel"* (4:4). The exact meaning of this phrase is not clear, as a comparison of various translations and commentaries will reveal. The two interpretations that appear most often in versions and commentaries are:

"control his body"
"acquire his wife"

The ambiguity exists because both phrases fit into the surrounding context. (Compare Rom. 6:13 and 1 Cor. 9:27 for teaching about the former reading; and 1 Cor. 7:2-5 for teaching about the latter.)

3. *"Lust of concupiscence"* (4:5). The phrase means, literally, passion of lust, and is translated "lustful passion" in the NASB.

4. *"Gentiles"* (4:5). The word is better translated "heathen," and is here clearly defined as people "which know not God."

5. *"Defraud his brother in any matter"* (4:6). The word "any" is not in the original text. The last phrase is correctly paraphrased "in this matter" (i.e., in the matter just discussed). Some interpret "brother" to mean any fellowman, as represented by this paraphrase of *The Living Bible*: "Never cheat in this matter by taking another man's wife." Others interpret the word as referring to a Christian brother, as the paraphrase of F. F. Bruce: "commits a covetous trespass against his fellow-Christian."

6. *"He therefore that despiseth"* (4:8). Paul is referring here to despising God's calling, just mentioned in the previous verse (4:7).

7. *"Brotherly love"* (4:9). This is "clan love," the love that is enjoyed by members of a family. Paul wrote much about Christian

2. F. F. Bruce, "The Epistles to the Thessalonians," in *The New Bible Commentary*, p. 1056.

love to churches in the Graeco-Roman regions (cf. 1 Cor. 3). "Christianity sprang up in a land [Palestine] and culture [Judaistic] where clan ties were strong and society was more corporate than individualistic. Not so the Graeco-Roman culture; hence Paul's constant emphasis on love."[3]

8. *"Study"* (4:11). Two different words translated "study" are used in the New Testament.
(a) meaning literally to use speed, not holding back (cf. Gal. 2:10; Eph. 4:3; 1 Thess. 2:17; 2 Tim. 2:15)
(b) meaning literally to be fond of honor (so used in Rom. 15:20; 2 Cor. 5:9; and the verse of this passage, 1 Thess. 4:11)

9. *"To be quiet"* (4:11). The word so translated means to be at rest (see Luke 23:56) and as used in this verse refers to a spirit of peace and tranquility that causes no disturbance to others (cf. 1 Tim. 2:2).

IV. FOR THOUGHT AND DISCUSSION

1. What do you consider to be some observable habits and deeds of a Christian who daily walks with God and pleases Him?

2. What helps a Christian to grow in holiness?

3. What does it mean to "know God"? (Consult such verses as Ps. 79:6; Jer. 4:22; 10:25; Hos. 4:6; John 17:3.)

4. Why should it be natural for Christians to love one another? Why is Christian love important? Consider the practical truths about love suggested by Romans 12:10; Hebrews 13:1-3; 1 Peter 1:22; 2 Peter 1:7; and 1 John 3:16-18.

V. FURTHER STUDY

Make an extended study of the doctrine of sanctification as taught in the New Testament.

VI. WORDS TO PONDER

This was the reaction of the unbelieving Greek writer Lucian (c. A.D. 120-200), upon observing the warm fellowship of Christians:

> It is incredible to see the fervour with
> which the people of that religion help each
> other in their wants. They spare nothing.
> Their first legislator [Jesus] has put it
> into their heads that they are all brethren.

3. Hubbard, p. 1354.

Lesson 7

The Lord's Return

The classic New Testament passage on the rapture of the church is part of the text of our present lesson. We observed in our survey study that the prominent doctrine in this epistle is that of the Lord's return. We noted, for example, that each chapter ends with a reference to that glorious event. We also observed that in 4:13–5:11, Paul expands on the doctrine to correct some mistaken ideas about it that were circulating in the church. Now it will be our pleasant experience to examine the passage in detail to learn more about that exciting reappearance of our Lord, an event that is closer to us than it was to the original readers by almost two thousand years.

I. PREPARATION FOR STUDY

1. The event of 4:13-18 is usually called the rapture. The word *rapture* is not found in the Bible, but it appropriately represents the phrase "caught up" of 4:17. (The Latin translation of the Greek word is *rapiemus*, hence, our word *rapture.*)

2. It should be pointed out here that when Paul wrote 4:13-18, it was the first time that specific details of the rapture were spelled out in Scripture, including Old Testament prophecy.[1] About three years later, when Paul wrote 1 Corinthians, he referred to the event in 15:50-54, calling it a "mystery." The source of Paul's knowledge about the rapture was "by the word of the Lord" (4:15). Possible interpretations of this phrase are:

(a) unrecorded sayings of Jesus (cf. Acts 20:35)

(b) a special revelation from the Lord (cf. 2 Cor. 12:1; Gal. 1:12, 16; 2:2)

---

1. See Charles C. Ryrie, *First and Second Thessalonians*, pp. 68-70.

3. One of the main differences between premillennialists who believe in a rapture before (pre-) the Tribulation period and premillennialists who hold to a rapture after (post-) that Tribulation arises out of the interpretation of the *action* aspect of the rapture (4:17). Pretribulationists believe that at the rapture the Lord does not come to the earth but only to the air and clouds above the earth, and that He returns to heaven immediately with the raptured saints. This may be diagrammed thus:

Pretribulational view of the rapture

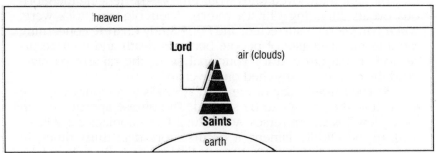

This view sees in the sharp phrase "caught up" the meaning of being transported from one place to another, which in this case is from earth to heaven. (Cf. Acts 8:39; 2 Cor. 12:2, 4; Rev. 12:5.)

Postribulationists, on the other hand, believe that the saints will be caught up to meet the Lord in the air, but that they will immediately accompany Him to earth.

Posttribulational view of the rapture

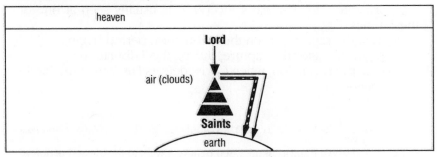

F. F. Bruce gives the background of such a view:

> When a dignitary paid an official visit or **parousia** to a city in Hellenistic times, the action of the leading citizens in going out to

57

meet him and escorting him on the final stage of his journey was called the **apantesis**; it is similarly used in Mt. xxv. 6; Acts xxviii. 15. So the Lord is pictured as escorted to the earth by His people—those newly raised from death and those who have remained alive.[2]

4. Paul wrote about the rapture mainly to comfort Thessalonian Christians who had been recently bereaved by the death of loved ones. (Read 4:13.) They did not have doubts that these would some day be resurrected. But they were grieving because they thought their loved ones would miss experiencing the glorious events attending Christ's return. Their big questions were, *When* will we be resurrected, and *how*? Study Chart K, concerning the intermediate state of people between death and their resurrection, as background for your analysis of the rapture passage. Read the various verses cited on the chart.[3]

5. The phrase "day of the Lord" (5:2) is a key phrase of the last half of the passage to be studied. The phrase appears also in these New Testament verses: Acts 2:20; 2 Thessalonians 2:2; 2 Peter 3:10. In the Old Testament, it occurs more than thirty times, in such verses as Isaiah 2:12; 13:6, 9; Ezekiel 13:5; 30:3; Joel 1:15; Amos 5:18; Zephaniah 1:7, 14. Read these passages, observing that the descriptions of this "day" are usually about judgment and war against sinners, a necessary purge before righteousness can reign. Saints are involved in this day in the sense that when the Lord brings judgment upon unbelievers, the saints are associated with their Lord in the victory. For example, the Millennium, issuing out of the Battle of Armageddon, may be considered a part of this "day of the Lord."

There are various views as to what period of time the day of the Lord refers to. The day's inception is usually seen at one of these times:

(a) at the rapture, when the Tribulation period begins[4]

(b) shortly after the rapture, during the Tribulation

(c) at the revelation, when Christ defeats His foes at the Battle of Armageddon

---

2. F. F. Bruce, "The Epistles to the Thessalonians," in *The New Bible Commentary*, p. 1057.

3. Before Calvary, the spirits of deceased believers went to the blessed region of Sheol, that part reserved only for God's people. After Calvary, only Sheol's place of torment (new name "Hades") remained, since thereafter the spirits of believers at death would go to paradise.

4. See J. Dwight Pentecost, *Things to Come*, pp. 229-31, for a description of this view.

58

INTERMEDIATE STATE OF MAN BETWEEN DEATH AND RESURRECTION

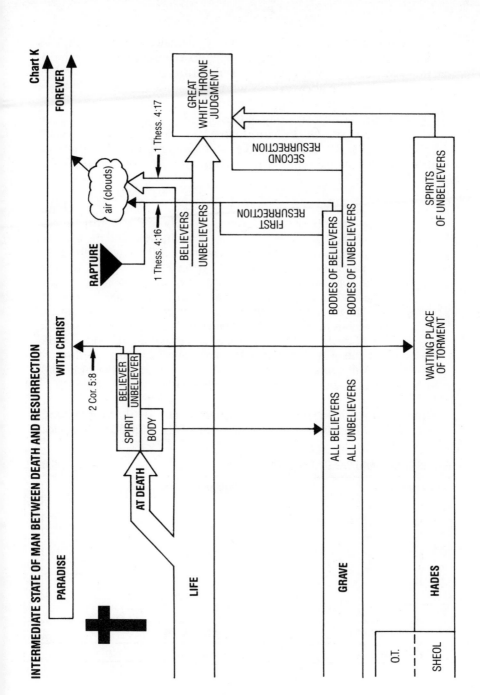

Chart K

59

You will want to come to your own conclusions concerning this identification. You may want to refer to commentaries for help. The view pursued in this manual is the third one noted above. Try testing each of the above views when you study the Bible passages containing the phrase "day of the Lord."

6. A similar phrase, "day of Christ," appears in the New Testament in these verses: 1 Corinthians 1:8; 5:5; 2 Corinthians 1:14; Philippians 1:6, 10; 2:16. This day will be inaugurated at the rapture of the saints. Merrill F. Unger compares "day of the Lord" and "day of Christ":

> Day of the Lord is the protracted period commencing with the Second Advent of Christ [second phase of Christ's return] in glory and ending with the cleansing of the heavens and the earth by fire preparatory to the new heavens and the new earth of the eternal state (Isa. 65:17-19; 66:22; II Pet. 3:13; Rev. 21:1). The Day of the Lord as a visible manifestation of Christ upon the earth is to be distinguished from the Day of Christ. The latter is connected with the glorification of the saints and their reward in the heavenlies previous to their return with Christ to inaugurate the Day of the Lord. The Day of the Lord thus comprehends specifically the closing phase of the Tribulation and extends through the Millennial Kingdom. Apocalyptic judgments (Rev. 4:1–18:7) precede and introduce the Day of the Lord.[5]

These distinctions are shown on Chart L. The Battle of Armageddon is the climactic event of judgment of the Tribulation period

DAY OF CHRIST AND DAY OF THE LORD Chart L

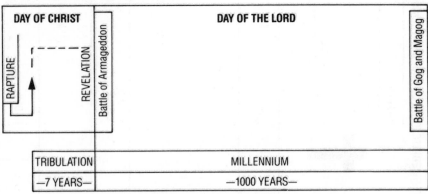

5. Merrill F. Unger, *Unger's Bible Dictionary*, p. 249.

that inaugurates the day of the Lord. Thus the day of Christ begins at the rapture, and the day of the Lord begins at the revelation.

7. Do not let the fact of differing views about the rapture cloud your perception of the spiritual lessons of the Bible text. D. Edmond Hiebert writes, "Equally devout and sincere students of Scripture will doubtless continue to hold different views on the question of the time of the rapture. . . . It is appropriate and proper that diligent effort should be given to the study of the evidence for a chronology of end-time events. But these efforts must not be allowed to lead to a preoccupation with uncertain details so that the sanctifying power of this blessed hope for daily living is lost sight of."[6]

II. ANALYSIS

Segment to be analyzed: 4:13–5:11
Paragraph divisions: 4:13; 5:1, 6

A. General Analysis

1. After you have marked the paragraph divisions in your Bible, read through the segment for early impressions. Underline in your Bible the key words and phrases that stand out.

2. The three paragraphs of this segment compose a natural and logical unit. Observe on the worksheet of Chart M the three phrases in the righthand column. Locate these in the Bible text and observe Paul's purposes in writing them.
   (a) "I would not have you ignorant"—teach new doctrine
   (b) "You yourselves know"—remind of known doctrine
   (c) "Therefore let us"—apply the doctrine
Complete the outline in the narrow vertical column beginning with *instruction*.

3. Compare the endings of the first and last paragraphs. Complete the entry on the analytical chart.

4. What is the main point of each paragraph?

B. Paragraph Analysis

1. *Paragraph 4:13-18*: Rapture
What verses cover the following subjects (record only the references):

6. D. Edmond Hiebert, *The Thessalonian Epistles*, p. 206.

61

RAPTURE	BLESSED RESURRECTION	4:13	I would not have you ignorant, nor sorrow
		↰ ever be with the Lord. WHEREFORE COMFORT ONE ANOTHER 18	INSTRUCTION
DAY OF THE LORD	SUDDEN DESTRUCTION	5:1	You yourselves know
LIFE OF WATCHFULNESS	SOBER CHALLENGE	6	Therefore let us
		↰ ———— WHEREFORE COMFORT YOURSELVES 11	

(a) comfort of rapture truth:

_____

(b) basis of rapture truth:

_____

(c) events of the rapture:

_____

What does Paul mean by the words "asleep" (4:13) and "sleep in Jesus" (4:14)?

_____

_____

List the various things that will take place at the time of the rapture. Note: the word "prevent" (4:15) means precede.[7] What is the emphasized truth of the phrase "so shall we ever be with the Lord" (4:17)? Does the phrase itself suggest location, activity, or state of existence?

_____

Compare this rapture event with the ascension story recorded in Acts 1:9-11. Do you think this supports the view that Jesus will come to the earth or only to the air at the rapture?

_____

Read 4:17 again. How does the verse impress you (without your reading into it any doctrine already known)?
    (a) that believers do not return to the earth at this time?
    (b) that believers return to the earth with Jesus at this time?
Read John 16:12-13. Is the intended comfort of 1 Thessalonians 4:18 dependent on your answer to the above question?
2. *Paragraph 5:1-5*: Day of the Lord
This paragraph is of two parts. What one short word separates the two?

_____

We have seen earlier in the lesson that the phrase "day of the Lord" usually refers to an aspect of Christ's judgment upon unbelievers.[8] Observe this to be the case here as shown in verse 3.

Read 5:2-3 again. According to the chronology of Chart L, does this "destruction" involve saints already raptured or unbe-

---

7. This is an example of an English word that has changed meaning since the time the King James Bible first appeared.
8. Obviously the "day of the Lord" is not a twenty-four hour day. It is an extended period of time, during which many events transpire, increasing in intensity until the end.

lievers living during the Tribulation period? What is the intended meaning of the metaphor "as a thief in the night" (5:2)? Is it unannounced, unseen, illegal, sudden, or some other meaning? Compare Matthew 24:43 and Luke 12:39.

Read 5:4-5 again. Note that the personal pronoun changes from "they" (5:3) to "ye" (5:4-5). Does "ye" mean believers? According to Chart L, where will saints be when the day of the Lord comes? What does Paul mean by verse 4? Consider this expanded paraphrase as a possibility:

> But you, brethren, are not of those who live in spiritual darkness, upon whom the day of the Lord will come without warning during the time of tribulation. That day will not overtake *you*, because you will not be there—you will be dwelling in light, in the presence of the Lord.

How would you interpret this passage, following the view that the day of the Lord begins with the commencement of the Tribulation period? You may want to consult commentaries on this.

3. *Paragraph 5:6-11*: Life of Watchfulness

Observe how Paul continues to use the metaphors of night and day in verses 6-8, as he had done in the previous paragraph. Compare the pronoun "us" of these verses, with "ye" and "they," as noted in the earlier verses. What is the repeated exhortation of this paragraph?

_____

Does Paul intend this to be applied to the coming of the day of the Lord (5:2) or to that event that is of immediate concern of the saints (the "us"), namely, the rapture (4:13-18)?

What triad of graces appears in 5:8?

_____

Observe how verse 8 leads into verse 9, which in turn leads into verse 10, as shown below.

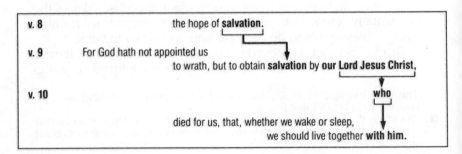

v. 8	the hope of **salvation.**
v. 9	For God hath not appointed us to wrath, but to obtain **salvation** by **our Lord Jesus Christ,**
v. 10	who died for us, that, whether we wake or sleep, we should live together **with him.**

Paul writes in 5:9 that God "appointed us . . . to obtain salvation." Is this a reference to the initial moment of regeneration, the continuing divine work of salvation in our lives, or the future consummation of our redemption?

What are the two commands of 5:11?

How do the preceding verses lead up to these?

III. NOTES

1. *"That ye sorrow not"* (4:13). Paul is not here telling bereaved saints not to sorrow over the death of loved ones. Jesus Himself experienced deep sorrow in hours of bereavement. Paul is writing that the Thessalonians need not grieve in the same way and to the same degree as those of the world, who have no hope of reunion. The Berkeley translation reads, "So that you may not grieve as other do, who have no hope."

2. *"With the voice of the archangel"* (4:16). The Greek reads literally, "With voice of archangel." The intention is not to identify the angelic chief, but to emphasize the *quality* of the voice, such as majesty and authority. (Michael is the only archangel in the Bible identified by name—in Jude 9.)

3. *"The times and the seasons"* (5:1). The word "times" here refers to duration (quantity); the word "seasons" refers to characteristics, or occasions (quality). In the short time that Paul was with the Thessalonians after their conversion, he was able to teach them the essential truths and lessons about last days, including the need for an attitude of expectancy that the Lord might return at any time.

4. *"Sober"* (5:6). This is not a reference to nondrunkenness but to stability and discipline in all areas of one's living. Other verses where the word appears are 1 Thessalonians 5:8; 1 Timothy 3:2; 1 Peter 1:13; 4:4; 5:8.

5. *"Breastplate of faith and love"* (5:8). The breastplate is the piece of armor that protects the body between the neck and waist. Compare the other figurative use of the word in the New Testament, in Ephesians 6:14: "breastplate of righteousness."

6. *"For a helmet, the hope of salvation"* (5:9). In Ephesians 6:17, Paul writes about the helmet of salvation. The helmet protects the head, the key part of the body. The name suggests this. A man's spirit and personality reside here, involving not only his intellect but also emotions and will. Here is where choices are made that determine a person's eternal destiny. Hence the helmet is called "the hope of salvation" (cf. Isa. 59:17).

IV. FOR THOUGHT AND DISCUSSION

1. One of the saddest phrases of the Bible is that of 4:13: "others which have no hope." Do you personally know anyone who admits that he has no hope of life after death? What will fill the desperate void of his heart?

2. Here are some questions related to the rapture event.

(a) What kind of body will you be given when you are raptured? Will it be similar to the one you have now? Will it be like Christ's resurrection body (cf. 1 Cor. 15:42-54)?

(b) Will unbelievers hear the shout, voice, and trump spoken of in 4:16?

(c) What kinds of gospel witness, if any, will unbelievers have access to after the church is raptured?

3. Do you think the rapture could take place at any moment, or are there events that must transpire first?

4. Why has God not revealed in Scripture the dates of last-times events?

5. What are ways in which Christians can comfort and edify one another concerning the second coming of Christ?

V. FURTHER STUDY

1. Jesus' illustrations used in His teaching and preaching usually came from rural scenes, such as farm, home, and nature. Paul, who was born and raised in the bustling, university city of Tarsus, drew most of his illustrations from cosmopolitan scenes, such as city life, business, and the military (e.g., 5:8). Study the following verses with this military backdrop: Rom. 13:12; 1 Cor. 9:7; 2 Cor. 6:7; 10:4; Eph. 6:11-17; Phil. 2:25; 1 Tim. 1:18; 2 Tim. 2:3-4; Philem. 2.

2. Study the book of the Revelation for references to the rapture, whether stated explicitly or implied.

VI. WORDS TO PONDER

The Lord Himself will descend from heaven with a shout (4:16, *New American Standard Bible* [NASB]).

Sundry Commands

The concluding passage of 1 Thessalonians is extraordinary among Paul's writings for its obvious compactness. Someone has described this as "little arrow-flights of sentences, unique in their originality, and pregnant in meaning." Paul could have easily expanded on each short statement or command, as he usually does in his epistles, but he chose not to do so here. Some might conclude that the apostle was rushed to complete the letter. Why not grant the possibility that this persuasive New Testament writer intentionally chose the abrupt lines to hold attention by such literary tools as variety and contrast?

I. PREPARATION FOR STUDY

The best preparation for this lesson is to review the epistle up to this point. For this, include a look at the survey Chart C one last time.

II. ANALYSIS

Segment to be analyzed: 5:12-28
Paragraph divisions: at verses 12, 23, 25, 28

A. General Analysis

Read through the passage to catch its tone. Then identify the main content of each paragraph. Compare your conclusions with this outline:

    5:12-22: Commands and exhortations for the Christian walk
    5:23-24: Assurances of the divine work
    5:25-27: Personal notes
    5:28: Benediction

B. Paragraph Analysis

1. *Paragraph 5:12-22*: The Walk of a Christian
List the many commands and exhortations of this paragraph. This is the core of your study of this lesson. Spend most of your time studying these important guidelines for acceptable living before God.
What different areas of Christian living are represented here?

_____

_____

_____

Do you see any groupings within the list?
Compare "we beseech you, brethren" (5:12) and "we exhort you, brethren" (5:14). In view of what follows each phrase, which is the stronger of the two? How many of the commands involve the believer's relation to other Christians? Observe the references to the three Persons of the Trinity in 5:18-19.
2. *Paragraph 5:23-24*: The Work of God
What ministries of God and Christ are mentioned here?

_____

_____ .

Note the threefold reference of spirit, soul, and body in verse 23. Does the Christian experience involve the total man?

_____

_____

Compare 5:23*b* with the similar phrase of 3:13.

_____

_____

3. *Paragraph 5:25-27*: Personal Notes
What word is repeated in each verse? What truths are suggested by the twofold designation "holy brethren"?

_____

_____

Observe the brevity of Paul's appeal for intercession (5:25). What does this teach?

_____

_____

4. *Paragraph 5:28*: The Concluding Benediction

The benediction is brief but inspiring. Christians often take for granted the ministries of Christ's grace in our lives. What would this world be like if this benediction applied to all people?

III. NOTES

1. *"Know them"* (5:12). The word "know" is used here as acknowledge, appreciate, and value.

2. *"Feebleminded"* (5:14). These were the fainthearted Christians, falling away under the pressure of such things as persecution.

3. *"Pray without ceasing"* (5:17). On the last two words, compare 1:3 and 2:13. The Greek word so translated was used in Paul's day to describe the lingering persistency of a hacking cough. "Just as a person with a hacking cough is not always audibly coughing though the tendency to cough is always there, so the Christian who prays without ceasing is not always praying audibly and yet prayer is always the attitude of his heart and life."[1]

4. *"Quench not the Spirit"* (5:19). The word "quench" is used of putting out a fire (Mark 9:49; Heb. 11:34; cf. Matt. 3:11; Acts 2:3). Paul is saying here, "Stop smothering the fires of the Holy Spirit." Perhaps some of the Thessalonian Christians were frowning on the outward manifestations of the gifts of the Spirit, such as prophesying (next verse).

5. *"Prophesyings"* (5:20). (Cf. 1 Cor. 12:28; Eph. 2:20; 3:5; 4:11.) Prophesying had to do with both forthtelling and foretelling. The command of 5:20 may refer mainly to the latter, a ministry that could easily be counterfeited. Verse 21 should be read as the other side of the coin of 5:20. Thus this paraphrase from *The Living Bible*:

> Do not scoff at those who prophesy, but test all things to see if they are true, and if they are, hold on to them.

6. *"Appearance of evil"* (5: 22). The word "appearance" means kind or sort, and is so translated in most versions.

IV. FOR THOUGHT AND DISCUSSION

1. What may be learned from 5:12-22 about the makeup and ministry of a thriving local church?

---

1. Charles C. Ryrie, *First and Second Thessalonians*, p. 80.

2. Joy is one of the fruits of the Spirit. What is your definition of genuine joy? Are you experiencing such joy in your own life?

3. What is the assuring truth of 5:24? How should this affect your daily living?

4. Can you think of any reasons for Paul's giving the emphatic charge of 5:27 to the Thessalonians?

V. FURTHER STUDY

Make a study of Christian joy as this subject appears in the New Testament. Suggested verses to consult are listed below.

1. Grounds of Christian joy: Matt. 5:12; 28:8; Luke 10:20; 13:17; John 8:56; 14:28; 16:22; Acts 15:31; Rom. 5:2; 2 Cor. 8:2; Phil.3:1; 4:4

2. Occasions of Christian joy: Luke 15:7; 19:6; John 4:36; Acts 5:31; Rom. 12:15; 15:32; 1 Cor. 13:6; 2 Cor. 7:16; Phil. 12:18; 2:17; 4:10; Philem. 7

* * *

THE CLIMAX OF PAUL'S THEME   **Chart N**

THE CHRISTIAN'S WORKING OCTAVE	CHRIST'S GRAND SYMPHONY
(1) Rejoice evermore	
(2) Pray without ceasing	
(3) In everything give thanks	The Lord himself
(4) Quench not the Spirit	shall descend from heaven with a
(5) Despise not prophesyings	**shout**
(6) Prove all things	**voice**
(7) Hold fast that which is good	**trump**
(8) Abstain from all kinds of evil	

A CONCLUDING THOUGHT

If we are sure of Christ's return, then our daily lives should show it. Let the diagram of Chart N impress this vital practical truth upon your heart and mind, as you conclude your study of 1 Thessalonians.

Lesson 9
Background and Survey of 2 Thessalonians

A couple of months after Paul wrote his first letter to the Thessalonian church, he decided to write again. This later epistle has been described as "a second prescription for the same case, made after discovering that some certain stubborn symptoms had not yielded to the first treatment."[1] But the epistle is more than that. It answers new questions that have been raised, and it extends Paul's earliest instruction and exhortation to deeper and higher levels. The keynote of the Lord's second coming, as taught in 1 Thessalonians, is also the keynote here, emphasizing the importance of such a doctrine in the lives of Christians.

The hope of the Lord's return has been called the polestar of the Christian church. It would be correct then, to say that the Thessalonian epistles are books of the polestar.

I. BACKGROUND

Most of the background of this epistle is common to that of the first letter and was studied in Lesson 1. You may want to review that lesson before studying the new material given below.

A. Author

Paul identifies himself by name in 1:1 and 3:17. The vocabulary, style, doctrine, and atmosphere all indicate that this epistle is as Pauline as the first letter.

---

1. R. H. Walker, "The Second Epistle of Paul to the Thessalonians," in *The International Standard Bible Encyclopedia*, V: 2068.

B. Origination and Date

Both Thessalonian epistles were written from Corinth during Paul's eighteen-month stay there, on his second missionary journey. The second letter followed the first by no more than a few months, or around A.D. 52. This was before the flare-up at Corinth recorded in Acts 18:5-17.

C. Immediate Occasion and Purposes

Whoever delivered Paul's first letter probably remained at Thessalonica long enough to view the conditions at the church and to bring back a report to Paul. The good parts of the report are the subjects of Paul's commendations in 2 Thessalonians. A negative report was the fact that the Christians were believing the false word that the "day of the Lord" had already come. This caused some of the believers to quit work, in anticipation of the shout and trump of heaven heralding the Lord's return. These were some of the things that Paul wanted to write about in a second, brief letter. So the purposes of the letter were (a) commendation and (b) doctrinal and practical correction.

D. The Two Epistles Compared

Differences and similarities of the two epistles are shown in Table 3.

Table 3

1 THESSALONIANS	2 THESSALONIANS
describes how the Thessalonians received the Word of God	mentions their progress in faith, love, and patience
teaches the imminency of the Lord's return	corrects misapprehensions about that event
comforts and encourages the saints	assures coming judgment on Christ's foes
concerns the church	concerns Satan, Antichrist, and the world
presents outstanding eschatological passage in 4:13-18	presents outstanding eschatological passage in 2:1-2
tells about the **parousia** (coming, presence)—4:15	tells about the **apocalupsis** (revelation)—1:7
presents the Day of Christ (cf. Phil. 1:10)	presents the Day of the Lord (2 Thess. 2:2)

It will be seen from these comparisons that the two epistles differ mainly over which phase of the Lord's return is in view. In 1 Thessalonians, the first phase (rapture, day of Christ) is the main subject. In 2 Thessalonians, attention is focused on the second phase (revelation, day of the Lord). Our study of the text of 2 Thessalonians will help us arrive at our own conclusions as to whether this above distinction is justified.

As a background for examining whether the two epistles are emphasizing two different phases of the Lord's coming, differences between those two phases are shown in Table 4.[2]

II. SURVEY

Follow the same procedures of study as in your survey of 1 Thessalonians. Brief directions follow.

Table 4

FIRST PHASE (RAPTURE)	SECOND PHASE (REVELATION)
Christ comes to claim His bride, the church	Christ returns with the bride
Christ comes to the air	Christ returns to the earth
the Tribulation begins	The millennial kingdom is established
translation is imminent	a multitude of signs precede
a message of comfort is given	a message of judgment is given
the program for the church is emphasized	the program for Israel and the world is emphasized
translation is a mystery	revelation is predicted in both Testaments
believers are judged	Gentiles and Israel are judged
Israel's covenants are not yet fulfilled	all of Israel's covenants are fulfilled
believers only are affected	all people are affected
the church is taken into the Lord's presence	Israel is brought into the kingdom

2. Adapted from J. D. Pentecost, *Things to Come*, pp. 206-7.

A. Making the First Readings

1. *First impressions*
a. What are your first impressions after reading the whole epistle in one sitting?

_____

_____

b. Does this letter appear to be intimately related to the first one? If so, how?

_____

_____

c. Do you observe any overall likenesses or differences when comparing the two epistles?

_____

_____

PARAGRAPH TITLES OF 2 THESSALONIANS　　　　　**Chart O**

2. *Paragraph titles*
Read the epistle paragraph by paragraph, using paragraph divisions shown on Chart O.

3. *Main subjects*
Make a list of some of the main subjects of the letter.

_____

_____

_____

Where is the most concentration of practical exhortation?

_____

KEY VERSE: **2 THESSALONIANS: HE HAS NOT COME YET**

"Stand fast, and hold the traditions which ye have been taught, whether by word, or our epistle" (2:15).

KEY WORDS:
Lord
lawlessness
revelation
thanks
sin

PERSECUTION	PROPHECY	PRACTICE
We give thanks—3	We beseech—1	We give thanks—13	We command—6

PRAY—1
KEEP ALOOF—6
WORK—12

"DO NOT GROW WEARY OF DOING GOOD" (13)

MAN OF SIN

THE LORD WILL STRENGTHEN AND PROTECT YOU—3

WORK . . . 3:12

STAND FIRM . . . 2:15

THE DAY OF THE LORD HAS **NOT** COME YET! 1-2

DON'T BE DISTURBED

PERSECUTIONS

COMMENDATION	CORRECTION	EXHORTATION
MANIFESTATION OF THE LORD IN GLORY	REVELATION OF THE MAN OF SIN	ACTION OF THE WORD OF THE LORD
—a comfort to the persecuted	—a revelation and consummation of the lawless one	—demands a severance of fellowship with evil and idle men
—a terror to the unconverted (8-9)		

LORD'S RETURN

Record references to the Lord's return

1   2   3

75

Scan through the epistle and note the places of Paul's prayers or benedictions in behalf of the Thessalonians.

B. Observing the Structure

1. *Introduction and conclusion*
How does the epistle begin and end? Compare this with the first letter.
2. *Chapter by chapter*
(a) What is the main content of each of the three chapters?

chapter 1: _____

chapter 2: _____

chapter 3: _____
(b) What is the first word of chapter 3? What does this suggest as to the structure of the epistle?

_____

_____

C. Survey Chart

Chart P is a survey chart of this epistle, showing the broad structure of the three chapters as they compose the whole unit. Study this chart carefully, comparing its outlines and observations with your own. Keep this chart in mind as you begin your analytical studies.
Observe the following on the chart:
    1. The epistle is basically of three parts, one chapter per part. Study the various outlines of content and purpose.
    2. Note the focal point: "The day of the Lord has not come yet!" Observe how it relates to what goes before and to what follows.
    3. Note the list of key words. Add others to the list. Note also the key verse. Choose one of your own.
    4. Compare the title given to this epistle with that of 1 Thessalonians.

D. Review

As you prepare to analyze the Bible text in the next lessons, keep the bird's-eye view of Chart P always in focus. A review of this lesson will be of help here.

Before the Rapture: Persecution

Paul's second letter to the Thessalonians begins on a bright note, commending the saints concerning their severe trials. "The very fact that the Thessalonians are suffering patiently on behalf of the Kingdom of God is in itself an assurance that one day they will be accounted worthy to enter into it."[1]

This chapter is background to the problem specifically mentioned in 2:2. Just how it is related is one of the things we will be studying in this lesson.

I. PREPARATION FOR STUDY

1. Recall the key prophetic passage of Paul's first letter (4:13-18). Paul clearly foretold the sudden (though not necessarily immediate) event of the rapture of the saints. Then he wrote about the coming, unannounced "day of the Lord," bringing destruction and travail (5:1-5). Whether the Thessalonians interpreted these two "comings" as happening at different times, they did associate tribulation with the day of the Lord. When a letter forged with Paul's signature reached them with the message that the day of the Lord had arrived,[2] they were prone to believe it, because of the severe persecution they were going through. But that raised a problem: if the day of the Lord had already arrived, what about the rapture that Paul had foretold in his letter? Had it taken place, and were they left behind? We will study the details of this problem in the next lesson. In this lesson, we will observe how Paul interprets

---

1. *The Westminster Study Edition of the Holy Bible* (Philadelphia: Westminster, 1948), fn., p. 378 (NT).
2. "By letter allegedly from us, as if the day of the Lord had arrived" (2:2, Berkeley).

the meaning and purpose of tribulation for saints before the rapture (cf. Heb. 10:32-39).

2. The word "tribulation(s)" appears twice in this passage. It should not be confused with *the* Tribulation period (or the Great Tribulation period), which will transpire between the rapture and the revelation (Matt. 24:21). Read the following verses, where the word has reference to various kinds of trials that Christians are called upon to endure in their daily walk: John 16:33; Romans 5:3; 12:12; 2 Corinthians 1:4; 7:4; Ephesians 3:13; 1 Thessalonians 3:4.

3. Ultimate judgment of all unbelievers will fall at the great white throne judgment. Read Revelation 20:11-15 for the description of this most awesome and tragic event. This is background to verses 8-10 of the present passage.

4. Paul writes of three different subjects in the three chapters of this epistle. Note the different time element in each:

chapter 1—before the rapture: persecution (tribulation)
chapter 2—before the revelation: Antichrist (man of sin)
chapter 3—how Christians should live now

This brief outline will help keep you on course as you make your way through this stirring epistle.

II. ANALYSIS

Segment to be analyzed: 1:1-12
Paragraph divisions: at verse 1, 3, 5, 11

A. General Analysis

1. Read the chapter through once, underlining strong words and phrases as you read.
2. After you have marked the paragraph divisions in your Bible, record the main content of each paragraph:
1:1-2

_____

1:3-4

_____

1:5-10

_____

1:11-12

_____

3. Observe the reference to grace at the beginning and end of the chapter. Note also that Paul writes of grace at the end of the other two chapters.

4. In your own words, what is Paul trying to establish in this opening chapter?

_____

_____

_____

B. Paragraph Analysis

1. *Paragraph 1:1-2*: Salutation
Compare this salutation with that of the first epistle.

2. *Paragraph 1:3-4*: Commendation
For what things does Paul commend the Thessalonians?

_____

_____

_____

Observe the words "groweth exceedingly" and "aboundeth" in verse 3. Compare this with Paul's earlier exhortation of 1 Thessalonians 4:1.

3. *Paragraph 1:4-10*: Explanation
The key phrase of this paragraph is "righteous judgment of God" (1:5). Paul illustrates "the fair, just way God does things" (v. 5a, *The Living Bible*), with respect to Christians being persecuted, as well as to the persecutors themselves. The full explanation of justice in situations of tribulation for Christians must take into account three parties, as shown on Chart Q.

Complete the diagram by recording the righteous judgments of God involving the persecutors and the Christians being persecuted. Note the words "revealed" (1:7) and "come" (1:10), as they are used in the descriptions. Is this a coming that involves only saints (such as the rapture), or is the unbelieving world involved as well (such as the second phase, the revelation)? How would the message of this paragraph have helped the Thessalonians in their quandary about how their tribulation related to the rapture event?

4. *Paragraph 1:11-12*: Inspiration
Analyze this prayer carefully. What inspiration would these words

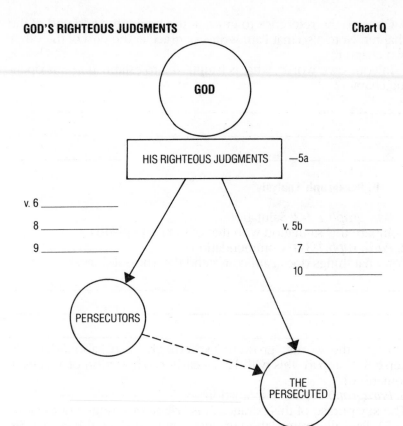

have given to the Thessalonians to continue in their patience and endurance?

_____

_____

On the Christian's calling, compare Ephesians 4:1-3 and Colossians 3:1-4.

III. NOTES

1. _"In flaming fire"_ (1:8). In biblical times, fire was often the symbol of divine presence, such as at Mt. Sinai and on the day of Pentecost. Compare these related references: Exodus 3:2; Isaiah 66:15; Daniel 7:10-11; 2 Peter 3:7.

2. _"Taking vengeance"_ (1:8). The Greek word translated "vengeance" means literally "out of justice." The Lord inflicts ven-

geance not "out of a sense of injury or merely out of a feeling of indignation. . . . The judgments of God are holy and right (Rev. 16:7), and free from any element of self-gratification or vindictiveness."[3]

3. *"Everlasting destruction"* (1:9). This is final ruin, a ruin that is not annihilation, and a finality that is endless because there is no restoration or recovery. Specifically this everlasting destruction is identified as separation from the presence of the Lord.

IV. FOR THOUGHT AND DISCUSSION

1. Paul never tired of expressing his gratitude to God for other Christians. And he also shared this with the Christians themselves. Do many Christians follow his example today?

2. The age-old question is, "Why do the righteous suffer, and the wicked prosper?" What is your answer? Does the passage of this lesson shed any light?"

V. FURTHER STUDY

1. One of the ministries of Christ is the judging of the souls of men. Read John 5:22, 27. Inquire into other New Testament passages that teach this.

2. Study the New Testament teachings about hell. "New Testament descriptions of the pangs of hell are numerous: 'furnace of fire' (Matt. 13:42); 'lake of fire and brimstone' (Rev. 20:10); 'outer darkness' (Matt. 25:30), etc. But none is more graphic than this picture (2 Thess. 1:9) of endless, utter exclusion from him who is life, light, and love."[4]

VI. WORDS TO PONDER

To those whom he has made holy his coming will mean splendor unimaginable. It will be a breath-taking wonder to all who believe (1:10, Phillips).

3. W. E. Vine, *An Expository Dictionary of New Testament Words*, 4:184.
4. David A. Hubbard, "The Second Epistle to the Thessalonians," in *The Wycliffe Bible Commentary*, pp. 1362-63.

Before the Revelation: Antichrist

This second chapter is the heart of the epistle; it is here where Paul treats the problem vexing the Thessalonian Christians. In chapter 1, he wrote, "We thank God for you," "We glory in you," and, "We pray for you." At 2:1, it is, "Now we beseech you," as the apostle plunges into the problem without delay.

The passage before us contains one of the New Testament's fullest descriptions of the activity and defeat of Antichrist, called the "man of sin" in 2:3. The chapter's main point is that the day of the Lord will not come until the Antichrist has first been revealed and worshiped by the world as God.

I. PREPARATION FOR STUDY

1. Because the Antichrist is a main character of this chapter, it will be helpful for you to read other passages of Scripture about him. (The Thessalonians knew about him from the Old Testament and from Paul's earlier instruction—see 2:5-6.)

Read the following: Ezek. 38-39; Dan.7:8, 20; 8:24; 11:28–12:3; Zech. 12-14; Matt. 24:15; 1 John 2:18, 22; 4:3; 2 John 7; Rev. 13:1-10; 17:8.

Various names by which this Antichrist is identified in Scripture are the little horn (Dan. 7:8; 8:9), the prince that shall come (Dan. 9:26), the wilful king (Dan. 11:36), the man of sin (2 Thess. 2:3), the son of perdition (2 Thess. 2:3), that Wicked one (2 Thess. 2:8), antichrist (1 John 2:18), and the beast out of the sea (Rev. 13:1-10).

John wrote about many antichrists in the world but singled out the Antichrist (1 John 2:18). This Antichrist is a real person, an emissary of Satan, the personification of evil and the culmination of all that is opposed to God.

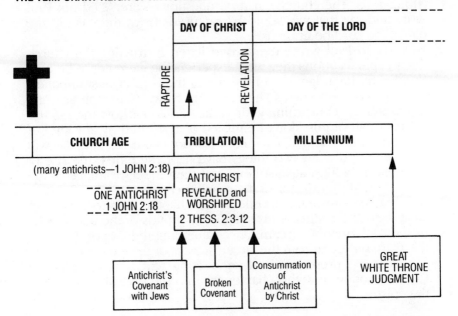

Chart R shows the temporary reign of Antichrist during the Tribulation period, as it is related to the two phases of Christ's coming—the rapture and revelation. You will want to keep this chronology in mind as you study chapter 2.

2. Two phrases of the King James text should be clarified from the start. "By the coming of our Lord" (2:1) means, "With regard to the coming of our Lord" (Berkeley). "The day of Christ is at hand" (2:2) should read, "The day of the Lord has come."[1]

3. Now let us reconstruct the background of 2 Thessalonians 2.

(a) In the first letter, Paul instructed the Thessalonians to expect a sudden rapture, when deceased and surviving believers would be caught up to be with Christ forever (1 Thess. 4:13-18).

(b) In the same letter, Paul wrote that the day of the Lord—a time of judgment for unbelievers—would come upon the unbelieving world unannounced, "as a thief in the night" (1 Thess. 5:1-3).

(c) After receiving that letter, the Thessalonians had continued to be sorely persecuted for their faith. False teaching was circulating that the day of the Lord had already come, bringing these

---

1. This strongly attested manuscript reading and translation is accepted by most commentators and Bible versions (cf. NASB).

tribulations. The church's natural questions were, "Did not Paul write and say that we would be raptured? How, then, could the day of the Lord be upon us?"

(d) So Paul wrote the second letter, instructing the church that the persecutions they were experiencing were not to be confused with the judgments of the day of the Lord against unbelievers. That was yet to be (2 Thess. 1:7-9). "Now," to paraphrase Paul in chapter 2, "concerning your confusion about how the rapture relates to all of this: don't be misled or disturbed by any kind of false teaching. The day of the Lord has *not* come yet. That day will not come until after two things have happened: first, the rise of the great rebellion against God, and then the appearance of the man of sin, the instigator of the rebellion."

(e) The aim of the apostle in this chapter, therefore, was "to clear away the confusion existing in the minds of the converts by further defining the circumstances attending the Day of the Lord; these are different from the circumstances of the Parousia."[2]

4. As you prepare to analyze the Bible text, review the survey Chart P, noting how this chapter fits into the overall structure of the epistle.

II. ANALYSIS

Segment to be analyzed: 2:1-17
Paragraph divisions: at verses 2:1, 5, 13, 16

A. General Analysis

Scan the chapter for general observations. Compare the first two paragraphs with the last two. What is the main subject of each paragraph?

2:1-4

_____

2:5-12

_____

2:13-14

_____

2:15-16

_____

2. C. F. Hogg and W. E. Vine, *The Epistles to the Thessalonians*, p. 245.

84

B. Paragraph Analysis

1. *Paragraph 2:1-4*: The Appearance of Antichrist
Does verse 1 sound like a reference to the rapture or to the return of Christ to the earth?

What precedes the coming of the day of the Lord?

How is the Antichrist described in these verses?

---

2. *Paragraph 2:5-12*: The Overthrow of Antichrist
Read verses 6 and 7 in a modern paraphrase, for clarification. (See *Notes* on the phrase "what withholdeth" and "he who now letteth will let.") Answer the following, on the basis of this paragraph.

(a) The Antichrist is alive in the world, with limited powers, before he is fully revealed (*true* or *false*).

(b) That which (or, he who) now hinders the Antichrist from full expression is clearly identified in the paragraph (*true* or *false*).

(c) At the appointed time, the Antichrist will be unveiled, able to perform miracles and deceive multitudes (*true* or *false*).

(d) Christ will eventually destroy Antichrist at His coming (*true* or *false*).
Which of the following two interpretations of 2:1-12 do you think is correct?

(a) Paul is teaching that the revealing of Antichrist will be a sign to Christians living on earth.

(b) Paul is showing that neither the rapture nor the day of the Lord has occurred, since Antichrist has not yet been revealed.
3. *Paragraph 2:13-15*: Exhortation and Instruction
What does this paragraph teach about:
sovereign election

---

salvation

---

sanctification

---

faith

---

calling

---

glorification

Compare Romans 8:29-30.
What is Paul's appeal in 2:15?

---

4. *Paragraph 2:16-17*: Benediction
Analyze carefully the different parts of this benediction. Record your observations. How do the last two paragraphs relate to the first two in a practical way?

III. NOTES

1. *"A falling away"* (2:3). This should be translated "the falling away" and has reference to the well-known apostasy of professing Christians, an aggressive and positive revolt against God, which will characterize Christendom in the end-time (1 Tim. 4:1-3; 2 Tim. 3:1-5; 4:3-4; James 5:1-8; 2 Peter 2:1-22; 3:3-6; Jude).[3]

2. *"Revealed"* (2:3). At the predetermined time, Antichrist, then a relatively unknown person, will be revealed to the world.

3. *"Son of perdition"* (2:3). This is the one "doomed to destruction" (cf. John 17:12).

4. *"What withholdeth"* (2:6). The words "withholdeth" and "letteth" (v. 7) translate the same word meaning "restrains." Various views are held as to who or what the restrainer is. Included are government, Roman empire, Gentile dominion, the Jewish state, the preaching of the gospel, Satan, the providences of God, and the Holy Spirit.[4]

5. *"Lying wonders"* (2:9). These "will be real miracles, but their purpose will be to deceive men into acknowledging Antichrist's spurious claim to deity."[5]

---

3. See D. Edmond Hiebert, *The Thessalonian Epistles*, p. 306.
4. See ibid., pp. 313-14, for a clear defense of the view that the restrainer is the Holy Spirit.
5. Hogg and Vine, p. 265.

IV. FOR THOUGHT AND DISCUSSION

List five practical spiritual lessons taught by the generally dark picture of the first two paragraphs, and five taught by the bright picture of the last two paragraphs. If you are studying in a group, let each member express his conclusions.

V. FURTHER STUDY

1. With the help of books on eschatology (doctrine of last times), study further the subjects of Antichrist and the Restrainer.
2. How would 2:1-2 be interpreted in line with the view that the day of the Lord begins at the opening of the Tribulation period? Is the imminency of the rapture jeopardized by this view?

VI. WORDS TO PONDER

Stand firm and keep a strong grip on the truth (2:15, *The Living Bible*).

2 Thessalonians 3:1-18

How Christians Should Live Now

Paul's last word in all of his epistles, before the closing salutation, is that of practical exhortation. The Word of God by its very nature is alive and active. It is a message of life and of living. The Spirit inspired Paul to devote the last third of this epistle to some practical appeals concerning Christian living, based on what he had already written. The following outline represents this general pattern of the letter.

1 COMMENDATION and ASSURANCE	2 CORRECTION and INSTRUCTION	3 APPEAL and INSPIRATION

I. PREPARATION FOR STUDY

1. Refer again to Chart P, to see how this third chapter fits in the overall structure of 2 Thessalonians.

2. Reread the verses just preceding chapter 3, in 2:13-17. How are the things written here an inspiration for consecrated Christian conduct?

3. Keep in mind as you study this chapter that Paul is still thinking about the Lord's return. His practical counsel on daily living applies as long as the Lord delays His coming (cf. 1 John 3:2-3).

II. ANALYSIS

Segment to be analyzed: 3:1-18
Paragraph divisions: at verses 1, 6, 16

A. General Analysis

After you have marked the paragraph divisions in your Bible, read through the entire chapter. Record the main content of each paragraph.

3:1-5

_____

3:6-15

_____

3:16-18

_____

B. Paragraph Analysis

1. _Paragraph 3:1-5_: Victorious Christian Living
What are Paul's prayer requests?

_____

_____

What keys to victorious Christian living do you see in this paragraph?

_____

_____

2. _Paragraph 3:6-15_: The Disciplined Life
What sins were some of the Thessalonians guilty of at this time? What may have brought on this situation?

_____

_____

List the commands of the paragraph.

_____

_____

Note Paul's example. What lessons can you learn from this?

_____

_____

3. *Paragraph 3:16-18*: Conclusion
Compare the benedictions of verses 16 and 18.

Note the appearances of the words "all," "always," "every."

III. NOTES

1. *"Unreasonable"* (3:2). The word means literally "out of place" and refers here to men capable of outrageous conduct.

2. *"Patient waiting for Christ"* (3:5). This translation appears to refer to Christ's return. However, a more accurate translation is "steadfastness of Christ" (as interpreted in NASB).

3. *"The salutation of Paul with mine own hand"* (3:17). Paul usually had an amanuensis write his letters (cf. Rom. 16:22). Then, at the end, he would authenticate the letter as his own by some words in his own handwriting. Paul said that this token, or sign, appeared "in every epistle" (3:17). This note is significant in view of the forged letter referred to in 2:2.

IV. FOR THOUGHT AND DISCUSSION

1. What are your reflections about these three evils?

(a) *Disorderliness.* The word "disorderly" in 3:6 means "out of rank." How does this affect the ministry of a Christian organization?

(b) *Idleness.* The principle of 3:10 is "no work, no eat."

(c) *Meddling.* The last phrase of verse 11 is accurately paraphrased thus: "not busied in their own business, but are overbusied in that of others."

2. "Stop fussing, stop idling, stop sponging, and stop meddling" are the red lights of this chapter. Do they apply to Christians today?

V. FURTHER STUDY

Discipline in the church is not common these days. Paul recommends temporary ostracism and admonition of a Christian brother for disobedience, to restore fellowship. Study other New Testament passages that teach this kind of corrective discipline.

* * *

PAUL'S CONCLUDING REQUEST

> Finally, dear brothers, as I come to the end of this letter I ask you to pray . . . first that the Lord's message will spread rapidly and triumph wherever it goes, winning converts everywhere as it did when it came to you (3:1, *The Living Bible*).

What a grand conclusion to the inspired correspondence of the apostle with the Christians at Thessalonica. D. L. Moody had the same heart burden for lost souls as did Paul. He once said, "I look upon this world as a wrecked vessel. Its ruin is getting nearer and nearer. God said to me, 'Moody, here's a lifeboat. Go out and rescue as many as you can before the crash comes.'"

The Lord Jesus is coming again (1 Thess.). He has not come yet (2 Thess.). May we His servants on earth be faithful until He comes.

Appendix: An Approximate Chronology of the Life of Paul

EVENT	SCRIPTURE	DATE
Birth		around the time of Christ's birth
Conversion	Acts 9:1-19a	A.D. 33
First missionary journey —Galatians written possibly at the end of the mission, from Antioch	Acts 13:1—14:28	47-48
At the Jerusalem Council	Acts 15:1-35	49
Second Missionary journey —the first mission to Thessalonica included —1 and 2 Thessalonians written from Corinth	Acts 15:36—18:22	49-52
Third Missionary journey —at least two visits to Macedonia (cf. Acts 10:1-3; 2 Corinthians 2:12-13) included —1 and 2 Corinthians and Romans written	Acts 18:23—21:17	52-56
Arrest at Jerusalem	Acts 21:18—23:30	56
Appearances from governors Felix and Festus	Acts 23:31—25:12	56-58
Appearance before King Agrippa	Acts 25:13—26:32	58
Journey to Rome and imprisonment —Colossians, Ephesians, Philemon, Philippians written from prison	Acts 27:1—28:31	58-61
Release from prison	cf. Philemon 22	62
Travels after release —1 Timothy (A.D. 62) and Titus (A.D. 66) written		62-66
Arrest	cf. 2 Timothy 1:16-17; 4:6-18	66 or 67
Second imprisonment at Rome —2 Timothy written		67
Execution by Nero		67

Bibliography

RESOURCES FOR FURTHER STUDY

Everyday Bible. New Testament Study Edition. Minneapolis: World
    Wide, 1988.
Hoyt, Herman A. *The End Times.* Chicago: Moody, 1969.
Jensen, Irving L. *Jensen's Survey of the New Testament.* Chicago:
    Moody, 1981.
New International Version Study Bible. Grand Rapids: Zondervan,
    1985.
Orr, James, ed. *The International Standard Bible Encyclopedia.*
    Grand Rapids: Eerdmans, 1952.
Payne, J. Barton. *Encyclopedia of Biblical Prophecy.* New York:
    Harper & Row, 1973.
Pentecost, J. Dwight. *Things to Come.* Grand Rapids: Dunham,
    1958.
Ryrie Study Bible. Chicago: Moody, 1985.
Strong, James, ed. *The Exhaustive Concordance of the Bible.* New
    York: Abingdon, 1890.
Tenney, Merrill C., ed. *The Zondervan Pictorial Bible Dictionary.*
    Grand Rapids: Zondervan, 1963.
Thiessen, Henry Clarence. *Introductory Lectures in Systematic
    Theology.* Grand Rapids: Eerdmans, 1949.
Unger, Merrill F. *The New Unger's Bible Dictionary.* Chicago:
    Moody, 1988.
———. *The New Unger's Bible Handbook.* Chicago: Moody, 1984.
Vincent, Marvin R. *Word Studies in the New Testament.* Vol. 4.
    Grand Rapids: Eerdmans, 1946.
Vine, W. E. *An Expository Dictionary of New Testament Words.*
    Westwood, N.J.: Revell, 1940.
Walvoord, John F. *The Rapture Question.* Findlay, Ohio: Dunham,
    1957.

COMMENTARIES AND TOPICAL STUDIES

Bruce, F. F. "The Epistles to the Thessalonians." In *The New Bible Commentary*, ed. F. Davidson. Grand Rapids: Eerdmans, 1953.

Hiebert, D. Edmond. *The Thessalonian Epistles*. Chicago: Moody, 1971. Highly recommended.

Hogg, C. F., and W. E. Vine. *The Epistles to the Thessalonians*. London: Pickering and Inglis, 1929.

Hubbard, David A. "The First Epistle to the Thessalonians" and "The Second Epistle to the Thessalonians." In *The Wyclifffe Bible Commentary*, ed. Charles F. Pfeiffer and Everett F. Harrison. Chicago: Moody, 1962.

Marsh, Frederick E. *Practical Truths from First Thessalonians*. Grand Rapids: Kregel, 1986.

Morris, Leon. *The Epistles of Paul to the Thessalonians* (Tyndale New Testament Commentaries). Grand Rapids: Eerdmans, 1957.

Ryrie, Charles C. *First and Second Thessalonians*. Chicago: Moody, 1959.